The True Reality of Sexuality

By Stewart A. Swerdlow
and Janet D. Swerdlow

Expansions Publishing Company, Inc.
P.O. Box 12, St. Joseph MI 49085 U.S.A.

Books by Stewart Swerdlow

Blue Blood, True Blood: Conflict & Creation
The Healer's Handbook: A Journey Into Hyperspace
Montauk: The Alien Connection
Stewart Says...
The White Owl Legends: An Archetypal Story of Creation

Books by Janet Swerdlow

Belief Systems Shattered
Decoding Your Life: An Experiential Course in Self-Reintegration
Life Support Group ™ Leader's Manual
Life Support Group ™ Member's Manual
Little Fluffs Children's Book Series
Practical Tips For Everyday Living Vol. I, II, III

Books by Stewart & Janet Swerdlow

The Hyperspace Helper: A User Friendly Guide
The True Reality of Sexuality

Copyright © 2005 Expansions Publishing Company, Inc.

Cover art: Thomas Dawson P.O. Box 753, Stn. Main Duncan, B.C., Canada V9L 3Y1
website: http://www.members.tripod.com/thomas_dawson
email: thomasdawson@shaw.ca

Cover design: Richard Beardsley, Quixotic, LLC

Typography and book design by Lorraine Sarich

Published by: Expansions Publishing Company, Inc.
                     POB 12
                     Saint Joseph MI 49085 U.S.A.
                     269-429-8615

ISBN 0-9740144-5-1

website address: www.stewartswerdlow.com, www.janetswerdlow.com,
www.expansions.com,
email: stewart@expansions.com, janet@expansions.com

We dedicate this book to each other,
and to everyone else who has the courage to explore
"The True Reality of Sexuality."
Love,
Stewart & Janet

Table Of Contents

Appendices

Introduction

To honestly explore the topic of sexuality on a personal level takes a balanced knowledge of Self, and a willingness to delve deep within some of your most sensitive discomfort zones. You must be willing to question some of your most basic belief systems, and where those beliefs originate – genetic, societal, family, religion, and beyond that...simultaneous lifelines and perhaps even programming?

You may find out that who you actually are differs quite a bit from your public personae. You may find out that you are not as integrated as you thought you were. You may find out that questions to which you had black and white answers have to be revisited.

In this book, we address many of the sexual issues, subjects, and questions that we see within our clientele on a regular basis. Some people will find this information shocking, perhaps almost blasphemous. Others will be more open and receptive, and will give it serious thought. Still others may read for curiosity sake. But the fact that you read the book changes you simply because the information is now within your frequency.

The book will be a sexual trigger for many people, so before each reading of the book, we highly suggest that you do the basic preliminary balancing and grounding techniques as taught in *The Healer's Handbook: A Journey Into Hyperspace* (Skybooks, 1998) and *The Hyperspace Helper* (Expansions Publishing Company, Inc., 2004). These include balancing your T-Bar archetype, spinning your chakras, using the ultimate protection technique, and placing the brown merger archetype at the pineal gland and in the root chakra for the purposes of best understanding and reading of this book.

If you find yourself sexually responding to the material presented, re-balance and re-ground yourself, put yourself in a deep brown, and take a break from reading. You might want to go for a walk, eat some heavier proteins, and/or even take a sea salt bath. When you go back to reading, remember to start over again with the basic preliminary balancing and grounding techniques.

We have tried our best to objectively present these sensitive topics so that you in turn may objectively evaluate our research. You may be surprised by your own reactions and evaluations. As always, give everything up to your Oversoul and God-Mind to help you reach your own personal conclusions.

Stewart & Janet Swerdlow

1

Sexuality - The Basis of All Creation

Everyone has a need to create. Everyone creates every day, in every moment. Each pathway through your life is an experience in creativity. You create through art, cooking, decorating, sports, hobbies, recreation, career, finances, and relationships. You create your inner and outer self; your inner and outer worlds. When you stop and think about it, you are in a constant state of creativity as you replicate the creative force of the God-Mind in this reality. You have a need to create because the God-Mind has a need to create. As above, so below.

Your physical body is the vehicle through which the soul-personality outpictures the creative flow into this reality. Every cell in your body constantly responds to this continual pouring of creative energy through it. It is no wonder that the root chakra band, the seat of creativity, is highly charged and responsive to this intense flow of energy throughout the entire system, as well as to stimuli from the outer world.

The sexual organs, located in the root chakra band, are the primary channel from the nonphysical realm to the physical realm. Because of the intense creative nature of humankind, sexuality is the number one subject at the forefront of the minds of most people. As blasphemous as it may sound, more people prefer to read about sexuality and body sensations than they want to read about God—this is just the way it is. Perhaps, when you look at the deeper picture, this is not so strange and unrelated after all.

When you understand how the God-Mind operates within the context of physical realities, you realize that sexuality actually does have a lot to do with God, although not in the same way that has been imprinted upon modern society. Physical sexual activity is a constant replication of the God-Mind's creative energy. Your preference of sexual type and format is a clue of how your soul-personality replicates that of the Creator.

The sensation of orgasm, which is the usual culmination of any type of sexual activity, is the lowest form of reproducing the sensations experienced by the God Force at the moment It creates All That Is. The release felt by God-Mind at the point of creating all universes, is what each person attempts to achieve when recreating his/her own little version of creation.

When you understand about the nature of reality on this planet, you realize that it is a symbolic representation of the nonphysical energies that created it. The ancient peoples worshipped God in the manifestations of the Father-Sun, a masculine energy, and the Mother-Earth, a feminine energy. The infinite long, warming rays of the Father-Sun allow for the limited abilities of the Mother-Earth to produce the life forms that find comfort, growth, and nurturing upon and in her.

Males, being symbolic of Father-Sun and the nonphysical, think of sex almost every few minutes. Females, being symbolic of Mother-Earth and the physical, use sex more sparingly as it can be more finite for them, especially since they can become pregnant which then curtails their physical activities.

Females have cycles, just like the Earth. The Earth has seasons that allow times for growth and dormancy. Women are born with a finite number of eggs that can be fertilized. Their fertility time is limited from the start of puberty until the time of menopause. Females can have multiple orgasms as a sign of multiple physical creations on the Earth plane. The menstrual cycle is twenty-eight days in length, exactly identical to the twenty-eight day cycle of the moon.

Males have no cycle. They can produce sperm from the time of puberty until the day of death. One ejaculate alone contains enough sperm to populate the entire planet. Males limit the frequencies of their orgasms since they need time to "recover" in order to be stimulated and ejaculate again. Even their seminal fluids need time to be regenerated. This represents the sine wave cycles of energy fluctuations and pulses. The male has unlimited sperm production while the female has limited reproductive abilities.

Female ovaries are round in shape, which is the hyperspace archetype symbol for "space" or "environment." Male testes are basically oblong, which is the hyperspace archetype for "time." When you place the ovaries and testes together, you have the symbols for space and time. These, then, are a function of a linear physical reality, since outside of the Earth plane physicality, there is no time or space. Both are an illusion of a physical universe.

When a male and female human have sexual relations with each other, what happens is a re-enactment of God-Mind sending energy to a physical reality for the purpose of manifesting something. Similarly, it is a symbol of the Father-Sun keeping the Mother-Earth fertile so that growth can occur. Both have the opportunity to also feel the orgasmic release energy that started all of this in the first place. Literally, a "Big Bang!"

Sexuality for humans is also a matter of polarities representing two energies coming together to create a third. This trinity forms an equilateral triangle, which is the hyperspace symbol for creation or perfection. Of course, since everyone is part of the God-Mind, the polarity and therefore, the sexuality of each individual can change depending upon need for experience. Everyone already has both male and female energies inside. Ultimately, all creatures are androgynous, because God-Mind does not really have a gender. God-Mind is *All One.*

In the same way, during sexual union the partners also become as *one.* They recreate the concept of a need to unify while in the process of creating. Re-create means to create again. What partners really do during sexual union is to re-enact the initial "thrust" of God-Mind in the process of creation.

When the words *"All One"* are placed together they become *"Allone."* Each *"I"* can represent the two sexual partners. When the two merge together, they become as one, and one *"I"* can be dropped. Now the word becomes *"alone."* This helps to illustrate why the God-Mind felt a need or desire to create something else from within Itself.

Look at the symbolism behind the sexual parts of the body. You have heard of the "Tree of Life" that was popularized within the context of ancient Jewish mysticism known as Kabala. The erect male genitalia can be compared to this "Tree of Life." It has a trunk with a wider head, or top. This "tree" has roots (root chakra) and gives its seed to the Earth to grow. Semen has the same sticky consistency as tree sap. Trees also release numerous seeds to the ground.

The female vagina can be compared to a pool or pond in which life flows. The vagina is connected to the uterus which is located in the sacral, or creative, chakra. Trees always grow around water. Without water there can be no trees.

Energetically and via thought-band, the uterus has its male counterpart in the prostate gland. The prostate gland prepares the sperm for ejaculation in the semen (seamen). The uterus prepares the fertilized egg for ejection and growth into the world. With birth, the new creation takes its berth in the world.

Foreplay is really the most important part of the sexual experience for most people. Because males can generally just think of sex and physically be ready for it, they sometimes forget or omit to please their partners, preferring to proceed directly to orgasm. Women prefer more foreplay because they are usually not able to be physically ready for penetration by the erect penis. They must be sufficiently stimulated to be moist enough so that sexual intercourse is comfortable.

Symbolically, foreplay is the building of energies within the God-Mind for creational purposes that become so powerful that it can no longer be maintained as thought. It must manifest in more than one reality in order to be fully expressed and fulfilled. The vagina is really a vortex that is used as a step-up transformer for the energies of both partners. During foreplay, the vortex is opened, not only into the body but into the connection with other realities where creation actually takes place. Preparing the female for male penetration is actually opening a vortex into the creative forces of this reality and beyond.

SEXUALITY - THE BASIS FOR ALL CREATION

Human breasts and nipples, in both males and females, represent the ability to nurture self and others. In females, it denotes the ability of God-Mind to physically sustain physical creation. In the male, it represents the ability of God-Mind to nurture the creative forces. This is why in both sexes, stimulation of the breasts and nipples causes excitement in the genital region, as a preparation for releasing the energies.

Keep in mind, that every sexual act of stimulation is based on the excitement of energies that go into building the universes. The physical body is composed of the same matter as the stars and planets, only in different arrangement and format. Stimulating the physical body opens the pathway on all levels for the creative energies to flow. Rather than kept locked in the creative chakra bands, the energies are "unleashed" and allowed to course through the entire system. The body becomes a conduit for the entire creative force to flow, an instrument of creation of the God-Mind within. This creative activity puts you in the flow, or frequency, of the creations of God-Mind everywhere. Each person is truly a microcosm of the macrocosm, and in sexual union each individual has the opportunity to feel, experience, and replicate the Original Act of Creation.

At the moment of orgasm, the thoughts that you are thinking have the potential to be thrust out for manifestation in this reality. When you consciously direct your thoughts at this point, you can consciously create that which you want to come to you. This is one reason why the controllers of the planet instigate so much sexual intercourse amongst people. They want to capture this creative force for manifestation of their own goals and purposes.

In today's society, most males only want sex for pleasure, while the majority of females equate sex with emotions and possibly commitment. Virtually no one on the planet actually thinks of how symbolic and spiritual sexual union is when performed with the idea of re-enacting the creative process of the God-Mind.

Can you imagine sexual union from the perspective of All That Is? How amazing the experience would be! Of course, this would be closer to the ideal of "making love." But, keep in mind that people cannot truly

15

"make" love. Love already exists as an emotion that you can use or not use as you allow. This is Free Will. Experiencing sexual union with someone you love is more appropriate.

True sexual union has to do with allowing someone to touch you in your most intimate places in the most intimate ways. This represents sharing your deepest thoughts and emotions with someone else, and thus with yourself. This means opening up and becoming vulnerable on many levels. Just as the female opens her legs and allows the male to penetrate her deepest, most intimate physical place (thoughts), the male takes his most vulnerable physical place (thoughts) and puts them into his partner. Together, they explore new levels of intimacy, trust, and companionship with each other, and thus reach deep within Self.

Within this context, think of the sexual union based upon the idea of creation. The sensations from foreplay are the buildup of creation energy to the point where it can no longer remain stable, so it then explodes into a creational burst that emanates into all realities. Imagine the power and fulfillment you will feel and know. At that moment, you actually become *one* with the creative process of God-Mind in conscious awareness. When you hold this feeling in mind always, think how wonderful your life can become!

Many people wonder about the frequency of sexual union and what is considered "normal." Only you know what is normal for you—each individual must go by how he/she feels as well as the personal satisfaction and fulfillment factor.

God-Mind is infinitely and constantly creating, always in a constant state of orgasmic release. To replicate this in the same way would require humans to have nonstop orgasms. The human body is not designed for this. As a part of God-Mind, your mind fulfills this through its incessant thinking—this is constant creation. As the thoughts build in your mind, the brain which is a device of the mind, responds by creating sexual hormones and chemicals in the body. As these fluids build, so does the sexual desire until you feel the need for physical sexual expression. The more and deeper you think, the more sexual you are physically. The inner world always manifests in the outer world.

2

Degradation of Sexuality

Because sexuality is the pervading theme in this reality of constant creation, it is an easy hook to use to control the mass consciousness. Rather than harness this creative energy flow for the upliftment and evolution of all, it is taken to its lowest energetic form so that humanity becomes enslaved and enthralled by the very vehicle that could provide eternal freedom.

If humanity "discovered" the true reality of sexuality, the controllers of the mass consciousness would lose their hold. Because men and women want to know what sexuality is, the controllers put out several versions for people to explore. So, there is no need to go within. Before anyone can even ask a question about sex, the answer is provided. The need to ask questions is stifled, thus people go on exploring the products of the controllers instead of their own innate sexuality in alignment with their Oversoul and Angelic Frequency contained therein, and the God-Mind.

The highest attainable level of sexuality that anyone can achieve, according to popular belief, is called "love." Love can be a part of sexual union, but it is still a different and neutral energy that may or may not be a part of sexual union.

The mass consciousness is conditioned to have sex on the mind, as defined by the controllers, practically from birth. This conditioning ensures your distraction from discovering the true purpose of sexuality.

You are told to think sexually, you see sexuality in the media that reinforces this, and then you buy sexy products that make you think and feel sexual. As the advertising adage says, "Sex sells."

You never see an ad with "ugly" people in it. The marketplace is filled with images of slender, sexual people in all kinds of seductive poses and expressions. There are subliminal images layered throughout the ads that distort the subconscious mind into seeing a sexual act or even genitalia. These subliminal messages stimulate the corresponding body part, thus planting the subconscious thought that this product, service, or place will sexually please you. You become obsessed with the thought of purchasing it. In this way, sexuality becomes a tool used against the people, rather than promoting it as a Godly act of creation.

Conversely, religion in the Western world uses sexuality as a precursor to punishment. Religion teaches that people are "born in sin" because of Adam and Eve "knowing" each other. Sex is thus linked to evil as well as eternal damnation to hell. Religions often teach that if you even *think* of sex, you sin against God! Wow!

This teaches that the very act and sensation of creation is itself a crime. This is tantamount to saying that the air you need to breathe is evil and wrong—what choice do you have? If you do not have sex, then there will never be more people, and creation will end. Yet the Bible says to "be fruitful and multiply"? Confusions abound.

Religions continue their twisted dialogues by interpreting this to mean that God wants people to only have a sexual relationship for the purpose of procreation, not pleasure. Some strict orthodox believers only have sex when the lights are out, there is a sheet with a hole between them, and they are fully clothed. Hmmm...somehow these religious-types seem to have the most children. They must have worn out a lot of sheets!

The pornography industry is yet another extreme, encouraging people to have sex all of the time with anyone (and anything!). Sexual acts in these ways desensitize the process of sexuality so that it becomes no more meaningful than a yawn or a sneeze.

DEGRADATION OF SEXUALITY

Sexuality is further denigrated by the words that are used by people in ordinary conversations, as well as by radio and television shows. Words such as boobs, hooters, honkers, tits, knobs, bazongas, and flotation devices for women's breasts only add to the mental imprinting that women are unintelligent objects to be played with by men and then discarded. Perhaps this has something to do with the 200,000 cases of breast cancer that are diagnosed annually in the United States alone.

The male sexual anatomy is also denigrated by words like dick, cock, shlong, rod, shaft, pipe, balls, and nuts. These words give the impression of aggression and hostility as well as something that has no mentality or thought process. In fact, most men will tell you that their genitalia have a mind of their own—some even go so far as to name them! In this way, men absolve themselves of all responsibility involving the sexual act.

Make a conscious effort to use the proper words that are uplifting and respectful when describing the sexual organs, activities, and members of both genders. This may take some focus in the midst of the daily bombardments designed to pull you down into the further degradation of society. But, think about it—why would you want to add to this cesspool of thought? Instead, work to turn it around by choosing appropriate words that help to instill the true reality of sexuality back into the mass consciousness.

3

Sexuality in Media

The media in the Western world makes billions in advertising by promoting promiscuous sex in such a way that people feel the need to emulate what they are shown. Brochures for exotic travel destinations in warm climates generally show pictures near an ocean or large body of water. Without fail, there is a photo of a man or woman standing under an arch of some sort. This may be a natural arch of rock near a beach, or an archway to an old city or building. The arch, of course, is a vaginal symbol subliminally which beckons the male to enter it, imprinting him with the idea, "come here and you will find sexual opportunities."

These brochures often incorporate photos of a man and woman in bathing suits lying on lounge chairs by an ocean or pool, holding hands or gazing at each other with their feet pointed toward the water. You cannot see their faces, only the backs of their heads. This symbolizes the womb before birth as the egg and sperm come together to create life. This photo subliminally sends the message of a sexual union that will create new life in one form or another.

One of the most common images used in the media for subliminal imprinting is that of a city or town with a steeple or spire in the background, and a dome or body of water near it. The steeple or spire is a phallic symbol, while the dome or water is a vaginal symbol. Placing the two of them together tells the mind that sexual union is promoted that may even involve ritualistic practices.

The phallic symbol has long been a representation of power and control. In ancient times it was depicted as a sword or lance. The phallic symbol is imprinted using such things as a tower, tree, spear, gun, and cannon—and the bigger, the more powerful.

All major cities are filled with stretching skyscrapers that reach to enormous heights, built to withstand any natural disaster. These cities are testaments to phallic symbols, showing the world its power. These cities have huge populations, indicating fertility rites. There is a continual global race to see which city or country can build the tallest skyscraper first. Interestingly, Asia, with its burgeoning population, boasts the largest number of tall buildings in the world. A big phallus equals a more fertile and larger population.

Car commercials are notorious for their sexual tones. Sleek, shiny cars (phallic symbol) speed quickly down long roads (vaginal symbol). Often these commercials show mountains (phallic symbol) with the cars entering dark tunnels (sexual penetration) then focus on the exhilarated expression on the face of the driver. Sometimes, the car sits in the dark on a wet road or driveway. The moisture on the pavement is reminiscent of sexual moisture.

Underwear ads use countless photos of semi-naked males and females in various self-touching poses designed to make people want to wear, and then quickly remove, these undergarments. The subliminal imprint is that whoever sees you wearing such a garment will instantly want sex with you. Spontaneous and frequent gratification is what the media as a patsy for the New World Order (N.W.O.) imprints upon society. Buy this and wear that, and your sexual desires and fantasies will all come true. Most people are so busy trying to emulate this lifestyle that they do not stop to question anything. Like good robots, they simply emulate what they are shown. They are so busy with these planned outer distractions that they do not question the true motivations of any of it, much less their own.

Male models are all similar in appearance with light brown to dark blond hair, with a noticeable absence of facial and body hair which is seen as offensive by advertisers. All have slender builds and medium stature. Females are also similar to one another. They are mostly blond with a few redheads and an occasional brunette. Most have small breasts and are almost too thin.

Advertisements in all forms showcase almost naked people, with the subliminal promise that by purchasing their products you will look like them. Of course, most, if not all of those models are artificially "enhanced" in some way. Some have makeup and padding in strategic places, while others have surgically installed implants to draw attention to body parts deemed sexually attractive. With technology, photographs are easily touched up to bring about the desired effects.

Most naked people do not look like the models in ads or those displayed in the pornography industry. Yet, the mass consciousness is imprinted day after day to strive for that look and to act like them. Young people are under the impression that it is "normal" to have many sexual partners and not stay committed to any one of them. They are told to have as many flings as they can before marriage—and even afterwards.

The media leaves people with the impression that everyone is sexually experienced, which is not true. There are many people in all age groups who have never had a sexual experience with a partner. The media also encourages some people to become sexually active before they are ready because they think that "everyone is doing it" and they do not want to be left out. Others have multiple partners for the same reason, even if they really do not really what they truly want.

Bodies come in all shapes and sizes, representative of the variety of mind-patterns unique to each individual. By artificially touting unobtainable bodies, low-self-esteem and self-worth issues are instilled at an early age. No matter how hard most people try, they simply are not going to look like the model in the photo—most people do not have access to plastic surgery, body implants, personal trainers, and some-times even personal chefs, hair and makeup artists, wardrobe personnel, and on and on, plus professional photographers who custom touch-up photographs.

People become so absorbed with the outside look that they forget about the inside. They forget that people are supposed to be unique; that is, not all look, dress, and sound alike. People only want the coveted look in hopes of increasing sexual attractiveness. Thus, people begin to compartmentalize their looks. Instead of seeing themselves as a package that starts on the inside and radiates outward, they tediously review one body part after another to determine what is "wrong" with it and how they can correct it with surgery, makeup, illusion, clothing, diet, or a combination of these.

When people do not like their bodies, they develop shame, disgust, embarrassment, and emotional distance. And, if someone feels this way clothed, think of how he/she feels unclothed! This is a guaranteed shut-down of discovering the true function of sexual union. With this mindset, it becomes easier to experience sex "for the moment" or because it "feels good." Going beyond this level of sexual activity means piercing mental and emotional blocks, as well as facing personal internal mirrors. With a mind-pattern of self-loathing since practically day one, most people simply cannot do this. It is easier to go with the seemingly easy-flow spirit of society that enjoys casual and shallow sex.

Even children's cartoons are often rife with sexual innuendos beyond a child's understanding. This begins the sexual imprinting of society's greatest resource at their onset of life. Female cartoon characters are often scantily clothed with tiny waists and huge bust lines, sometimes even accentuating nipples through the clothing.

Many situation comedies are blatantly sexual, with British shows in the 70s leading with many overtly sexual double entendres, such as their use of words like "pussy" and "munching."

All of these advertisements and television shows are designed with one thing in mind—to exploit the creative, or sexual, energy of each and every member of society. They are designed to jumpstart the energy, then rev it up so that it courses through the body in such excess that it can be technologically "captured" and used against the people. What people give out must come back to them, including sexual energy.

In addition, many items are radionicly imprinted to psychically reach out and grab people. This especially includes tobacco products, alcohol, pornography, and gambling devices, from lottery tickets to slot machines. Once the creative chakra is open, it is easy for astral entities and forces to enter, attach to, and/or overshadow the physical body and even the mind. Many people with addictions to these things are influenced in these ways.

Once the sexual chakras are thus stimulated, people look for a way to release, or relieve, themselves of this energetic buildup. This leads many people to choose incorrect partners who do not match their frequencies. From these relationships people develop low self-esteem and loss of intimacy. Many of these sexual unions bring children into the world without thinking of genetic consequences and future parental responsibilities.

Children born of these conditions are imprinted with the same mind-pattern at birth as their parents, thus perpetuating the cycle. There is also less bonding between mother and child, much less father and child, creating a society of emotionally isolated individuals who make great worker bees, but do nothing to upgrade the collective consciousness. The media is leading people toward one global look, one global sexuality, one global mind-pattern. The few that dissent are inconsequential. The sheep are being led.

4

Feminized Males/Masculinated Females

As revealed in *Blue Blood, True Blood*,* androgynous Reptilian beings were here millennia before the hybrid human/Reptilians took over the surface of the Earth via religion, ritual, war, politics, economics, and the improper use of sexuality. The belief system of the hybrids is based upon their androgynous ancestry. Therefore, they work to create a society which leans toward androgyny. For this reason, the N.W.O. promotes bisexuality and homosexuality as a normal lifestyle.

Individuals are encouraged to look like sexless beings with sexual overtones. "Genderlessness" is encouraged. Look at futuristic movies where men and women wear similar clothing with similar hairstyles, and even use similar makeup and jewelry. Often it is difficult to tell which is male and which is female. This is what is being planned for our society.

In its own way, this is a natural occurrence, as God-Mind Itself is neither male nor female, but contains both. In this dual reality, however, to maintain the correct polarities, there is a reason why there are two genders. This allows each soul-personality who is in a male body to explore the masculine energy of God-Mind and the females to explore the feminine qualities of God-Mind. As a male/female couple, they are move actively able to bring in and replicate the creative forces of the God-Mind.

*(*Blue Blood, True Blood: Conflict & Creation* by Stewart A. Swerdlow, Expansions Publishing Company, Inc. Copyright 2002.)

This "de-feminization" began with the Women's Liberation Movement which basically began to tell women that they were "just as good as men" and then proceeded to teach them how to emulate men. Feminine qualities that were non-income producing began to lose their prestige. For example, nurturing the family—leading to the break-up of the family and placing newborns and infants in daycare; sewing and handcrafts—breaking down traditions and unique individual mind-patterns in favor of manufacturing firms; and cooking skills—leading away from whole foods into value-added products prepared outside the home.

Then women began to "ask" to work outside the home, leading to an increased work force, more material consumption, and eventually more slave labor that was consumption-oriented. From there, women "asked" to be able to join the military, and so on and so forth. Women did not take the time to explore the true female energy. They only saw that men were treated better by society. Rather than create their own unique niche, they went after the niche held by men. Of course, the glass ceiling still exists, but not just to women but to all persons who are not part of the 13 ruling families of the Earth. Women were distracted from this detail.

Hysterectomies were the "surgery of choice" for several decades for women. Effective birth-control, plus women did not have to deal with monthly cycles. Some women even hoped that their doctors would say the "H" word to them, wanting the surgical procedure. With the advent of birth-control pills to regulate monthly cycles and prevent pregnancy, women became more tolerant of their monthly cycles, regardless of the medication's side-effects.

Now, there are pills that suppress the menstrual cycle for a few months. Next there will be pills that permanently abolish menstrual cycles, and women will be thrilled when that day happens. On the horizon are artificial wombs—taking away the bonding that goes on between mother and unborn child. Again, people will be thrilled—they can continue to work and women will not have to worry about body changes.

They will be able to take hormones to stimulate breast milk should they so desire, but most will opt for formulas as breastfeeding becomes increasingly "old-fashioned." Just as breastfeeding imprints the baby with the mother's mind-patterns and enhances parent/child bonding, formulas can be imprinted with the N.W.O. agendas and enhance slave/owner bonding. An army of genderless soldiers eager to conquer space with extended periods away from "point of origin" (one cannot say family) is in the developmental stages.

Women are encouraged to develop their muscular body structures. Pregnant women are encouraged to physically exert themselves beyond what is safe for them and their babies. Even sports like bowling, skiing, and jogging are considered "safe" by current medical standards. Again, if it feels good, or even if you do it just because you can, women are given the go-ahead.

Female models are shown with slim, boy-like figures with small, almost non-existent breasts. Women are encouraged to have short hair, some women sporting crew cuts and shaving their heads. Women are encouraged to dress in men's underwear and shirts. Jeans are supposed to be unisex. When a woman uses cosmetics, she is encouraged to create a "no makeup" effect. Working women are encouraged to adopt the business attire of their male counterparts. The professional woman dresses in business suits with little makeup and low-heeled shoes. Blue-collar working women wear pants and shirts.

As the polarity in women is changed to bring out their masculine energy, males are responding by bringing out more of their feminine energy. Young men are starting to look more like teenage girls instead of young men as they are encouraged to be slender, svelte, and narrow-waisted, with little or no body hair, except for the pubic area. Emphasis is on being slim and toned rather than on large muscles and bulk. Many men choose to grow their hair long and styled.

Even the clothing males wear today shows a feminine flare. Styles include more color, shoulder bags, feminine-type shoes, and even makeup. This is reminiscent of Ancient Egyptian and Greek cultures where the males wore the makeup and wore dress-like togas and robes.

Men are encouraged to tone down their aggressiveness, while women study how to be more assertive. Males are taught to be more gentle and passive with others. Some stay home while their female mates are the major income producers. Many share equally in household chores.

Men look more like women and women look more like men. Many times it is difficult to tell not only from the back, but also from the front, if people are males or females. Couple this with androgynous names such as Jamie, Kim, Lee, Tony, Madison, Chandler, Chris, Bobbie/Bobby, Danny/Dani, and so forth, and it can be difficult to know if you are speaking to a male or female. In addition, females are given more male names now, and last names are becoming popular as middle and first names.

Because God-Mind must always be in balance, taking one energetic quality away from one of the sexes means the other picks it up. This is like mixing hot water into cold, or vice verse. The final product is an equalized version of the two additives. To maintain balance, a feminized male is often with a masculinated female. He is attracted to the male qualities that he lacks, and she is attracted to the feminine qualities that she lacks. On some level, there is always that need for the dual polarity that exists on this Earthly plane of existence.

This mixing of the polarities within one body weakens and confuses the body itself, which ultimately builds itself around the mind-pattern of the soul-personality that inhabits it. On some level, the body consciousness does not know if it is male or female, and works against the mind-pattern to try to correct the imbalance. The end result is that the soul-personality cannot fully function as it needs to in this reality.

Some day, there will be a natural return to androgyny through the evolution of the soul-personality with the mind-pattern leading the way and the physical following. But what is happening now is that there is forced androgyny of the body with the mind-pattern following. This is another example of a Universal Law being subverted.

5

The Energetic Skeleton

One of the functions of the sexual energy within the human body is to help keep the psychic energy of the body flowing. The psychic energy is the energy that runs the physical body. This energy runs your digestive, circulatory, and respiratory systems, for example. Psychic energy is what you use when you walk and talk. Psychic energy is your own personal energy that your soul-personality uses while in this reality in a physical body.

The body actually grows around the psychic energy flow. This is one reason why babies and children have so much energy. The psychic energy actually flows beyond the boundaries of the physical body. While the body is building, children feed off of this energy. The stronger the flow of psychic energy in and through the growing child, the more active the child.

The psychic energy flow follows a path through the physical body often referred to as "meridian lines." These are the lines that acupuncturists and acupressurists work with to stimulate the natural health of the physical body. The meridian lines are an energetic support structure for the physical body is like an energetic skeleton. The health of the body is dependent upon the dynamic continual flow of the psychic energy through these meridians.

Because of life's experiences and the emotional aftermath, the thought-forms of experience gather strength and energy, settling into this energetic skeleton. Then, the thought-forms move into the physical body, until finally they slow down, disrupt, and eventually completely stop the psychic energy flow through this energetic support system.

Sexual activity actually aids the health of the energetic skeleton, which is the body's support system. The psychic energy "pools" at the base of the spine, in the root chakra area. Orgasmic release "jumpstarts" the energy, sending it out through the physical body, thus aiding the natural flow. The more intense the orgasm is, the more intense the "jumpstart." This pushes the psychic energy through the accumulating thought-forms, thus opening and re-setting the energetic skeleton.

If you allow a continual accumulation of thought-forms to settle into the body, it becomes increasing difficult to jumpstart the energetic skeleton through sexual activity. This is when a person needs additional help in maintaining the health of the body, and usually starts seeking out some kind of healthcare practitioner to aid the process.

The physical bodies of people who do not have a lot of sexual activity actually become denser as the flow of the energetic skeleton slows down. A backup of energy occurs where the thought-forms are most accumulated, creating illness and poor health in a particular body organ, or in its function. When the energy cannot flow through the body at all is when the organ dies. In extreme cases, the entire physical body dies. At this point the energetic skeleton is no longer necessary and ceases to exist within the physical body.

Regular sexual activity helps to maintain the health of the energetic skeleton, which in turn aids the health of the physical structure which is built around it. You can also use the following *Green Psychic Energy Flush* exercise to help maintain the energetic skeletal system between sexual activity.

Green Psychic Energy Flush

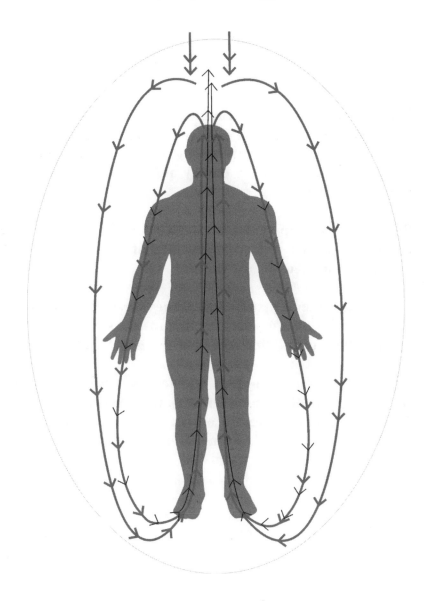

Purpose: To oxygenate, regenerate, & open the flow of psychic (personal) energy.

Directions
Green Psychic Energy Flush

From the top of your head, breathe in medium green from your Oversoul, bringing this color all the way down the outside of your body to the bottom of your feet.

Bring this green up through the bottom of your feet, permeating each and every cell of your being, flushing out all that you no longer need as it permeates the cellular structure on all levels. Feel the tingling of the energy as it moves through each section/cell of your body.

Bring the green up through your legs, torso, neck, and out through the top of your head, releasing all that you no longer need out the top of your head.

Allow the green flush to continue down through your shoulders, flowing down your arms, and out your fingertips, continuing to flush out all that you no longer need.

Repeat the cycle as long as you feel necessary, flushing, oxygenating, regenerating, and opening up your psychic energy lines as it flows, continually releasing all that you no longer need up through the top of your head to your Oversoul.

6

Sex For One

Sex for one is actually a very important process. This is a replication of the way that God-Mind produced creative energies in The Beginning. As previously stated, in The Beginning, God-Mind was *All One*, or, "*Alone*." Therefore, the only way for the God-Mind to excite Itself was via Self-stimulation.

As a microcosm of the macrocosm, sex for one also involves Self-stimulation, commonly referred to as masturbation. From a personal perspective, masturbation can be used to explore and understand the sexual nature of how one's own body works, functions, and feels. Why is it okay to physically self-explore all parts of your body except your own genitalia? You are taught that a partner can do this, but you may not? This does not make any logical sense.

Males are more likely to explore their genitalia simply because it is much more accessible and prominent on their bodies. Females are less likely to explore their bodies because so much of it is not so easy to view. Because of the monthly menstrual cycle, women may associate their genitalia with blood, discomfort, and uncleanliness.

The practice of masturbation goes against almost every religious and moral teaching. Religion, followed closely by the majority of parents, teach children that "touching yourself" is undesirable behavior and shameful. This leads to the guilt that most people feel, along with fear of what happens as a consequence, ranging from going blind to body parts falling off. Society indoctrinates its young to police itself in the privacy of their own homes.

There is a reason for this. The powers-that-be do not want the masses to understand this concept and practice it, out of fear that people will develop an energetic power base. Masturbation is a powerful force related to Sexual Magick Ritual. With this knowledge, each individual would be extremely uncontrollable. In addition, masturbation by specifically programmed people may interfere in their programming process.

To properly masturbate, you must truly care for yourself. People with low self-worth issues, or who are in a depressed state, most likely self-stimulate as a substitute for a sexual/emotional relationship with another person, or for a few fleeting moments of physical pleasure, or simply to release pent-up tension—or perhaps a combination of all of these reasons.

As disciplined as it might seem, no one should induce self-love unless you really do love yourself. When you are in balance, you do not "need" anyone else. Everything you ever need, want, or must know is already inside. The question is simply a matter of "if" and "with whom" you wish to share your life. This other person also already has every-thing inside of him/herself that he/she ever needs or wants. No other person, place, or thing can ever complete you because you are already complete.

Just as a "one-night-stand" can leave you feeling empty and unfulfilled, so can masturbation for the incorrect reasons also leave you feeling empty and unfulfilled. Both can leave you with feelings of shame, guilt, and fear. When you feel a need to release pent-up sexual energy, release these thoughts up to your Oversoul. Determine what you feel and why. Sometimes, meditation and visualization is a better energetic release of this pent-up power.

Recognize that sexual energy *is* a real power. The mind produces it for the body to use as a creative force in physical reality. Remember that a single orgasmic release can create universes. If you are in a negative state of mind when you masturbate, what will you create?

There is a real distinction between actualized self-love and narcissism. The latter involves having an egotistical adoration of the body image, and not what has created it. Therefore, masturbation with narcissism is like worshipping an idol. Plus, when you think like that, you cannot appreciate anyone else, so establishing healthy relationships of any kind become a major issue. When you think about it, both male and female sexual organs have become objects of worship, not only in sexual ritual, but in media and advertisements.

When a person feels that the need to masturbate several times per day, this may be the result of serious psychological or programming issues. A specifically programmed person may feel a need to reach orgasm in order to satisfy his/her handlers. Many involved with prostitution have this scenario involved.

From a psychological point of view, multiple daily self-stimulations may be the result of extremely low self-worth, resulting in a need to comfort oneself, very much in the same way that another would use food or alcohol. In this case though, the mind-pattern shows a person who has a problem with his/her own creative issues that he/she feels are diminished or unproductive.

As with all things, the process of masturbation is neutral. It is up to the individual to learn to use the released energy correctly.

7

Finding The Correct Person

For most people, finding the correct person for a sexual relationship for the correct reasons seems like an insurmountable task. Traditionally, this is more of an issue for women who most often consciously seek emotional attachment with a partner, while traditionally men simply want to have sex with the most beautiful person of the moment for the sake of having a sexual relationship.

This is changing as women are becoming increasingly content with sexual relationships without commitment, and men, after many emotionless sexual encounters are looking for emotional attachments. All of this is reminiscent of a popular country song that says, "looking for love in all the wrong places, looking for love in too many faces." This is exactly what many people feel after plying the meat markets of the singles scene for many years.

Because many single people say that they absolutely cannot meet the "right" person, they have given up trying. Instead, they seek immediate gratification, knowing that is all that is expected by both parties. How sad.

At the same time, many married people, or people in long-term committed relationships, often state that they are fed up with their partner. These people go outside the relationship to find fleeting excitement on the side. Some simply resolve themselves to their lives. Others attempt to satisfy their emotional needs with antidepressants, alcohol, and/or overeating. How sad again.

In addition, the media constantly provokes stimulation of the genitalia, creating a dam of sexual energy waiting to be released. This means that people often couple with the most convenient person for sexual release only. People may try to justify it in their minds as "love" or a myriad of other excuses, but the truth is that people are simply looking for others for sexual release. This perpetuates the "quick fix" cycles that lead no where except a downhill spiral. The same thing can be accomplished via masturbation, or passing the excess sexual red energy up to your Oversoul which in turn can hold the sexual energy for you until the appropriate time.

Too many people feel isolated and lonely, even when they are with others. Great care has been taken to break down the emotional bonds between people on all levels, replacing love, honesty, and trust with suspicion, competitiveness, combativeness, and general aggression. All these mind-patterns are imprinted upon people at an early age via society and hence, the family.

Even with all the attempts, and successes, of emotional bond-breaking, people still seek emotional bonding. The issue now is that these self-destructive imprints are layered on top of everything else. This neatly sabotages most attempts to bond with other people. Rather than cast off these imprints, most people merely label them "the other person's fault" and go from one relationship to the next, hoping beyond hope that the correct person magically appears.

This game of chance wears people out, so that eventually they "settle" for one-night stands, relationships they know will not last, or relationships in which they hope that the other person will change into the love of their life. Some think that no one will ever love them, so if they find someone who does, they grab this person. Some people see others coupled, and because they do not want to be a loner, they couple with someone simply for social reasons. Others partner for money, to have a family, because they are getting older, etc. The conscious reasons for choosing a partner are too many to enumerate. Most people are conditioned to think in quick-fix, short-term ways. The Illuminati, who are long-term planners, love this about humans. This mentality ensures and re-enforces a continuation of emotional bond-breaking.

Rather than go for the "quick-fix," which in most cases does not work, it is important to take some time to work on yourself. When you work on yourself, then the person who best reflects you automatically is pulled to you through the strength of your mind-pattern. If you are in a panic to bring in a partner, that panic energy will pervade the relationship and ultimately destroy it.

If you want to end your own suffering within relationships, then, as with all things, start with you! The more order that you can create within yourself, the more order will be reflected back to you within your relationships. When you are truly willing to grow within your own personal and Oversoul matrix, then the strength of this mind-pattern automatically draws the same type of partner to you. Once you are at this point, then you can truly begin the next level of intimacy that can only be accomplished with a correct partner.

Finding the correct person for the correct reason is not merely a physical agenda, although when you find the correct person, most likely there will be visual appeal. Recognize that beauty may be defined differently for each person. Even the color of hair may make a difference. As a general rule, women are more willing to overlook the physical because they seek an emotional and mental partner. Men may emphasize the physical appearance before seeking an emotional and mental partner. For a sexual encounter to be wonderful for both parties, a balance of mental, emotional, and physical attraction is important.

Some people still believe that the size of male genitalia or female breasts is important. The media reinforces this, consistently telling you in a myriad of ways that this is what the opposite sex seeks. This especially feeds people with self-worth issues who may already be criticizing their external appearances. Someone once said, "it's not the size of the wand, but the magic within." This can apply to many situations, although this person was specifically referring to male genitalia.

The truth is, it really is what you do with what you have, not the size of it. Small men and women can overpower much larger opponents. Young children give advice to those with more experience. Appreciate who you are and how you appear, and once you resolve this internal issue, then the strength of your mind-pattern will attract the correct partner for the correct reasons.

Loving and accepting yourself unconditionally attracts a person who feels the same and acts accordingly. Then, all will be perfect in every way, including sexually. Of course, this requires a lot of work on each person's part. Unconditional love, although always available, is not easy to actualize when you are imprinted to expect conditional love.

Once you find the correct person, stay loyal to that person in your intimate relationships, meaning mental, emotional, and physical. Too many energy imprints spoil the connection. You may see someone else and fantasize about him/her. But the reality is that most likely he/she is just like your current partner (or worse) with a different exterior. Why exchange one for the other? What do you gain? Why make a horizontal move, or worse, why risk a backward move?

When you do the *Golden Altar** release work, and/or your Oversoul work, you will eliminate the mind-patterns that attract incorrect people. Be persistent and consistent with your release work!

Once you attract the correct person, do not ruin it by falling back on old mind-patterns that sabotage relationships. This takes effort and work on your part. If something is yours, you cannot lose it. However, this does not mean that you dangle it close to the edge. Do not take advantage of the person you are with, and do not compare yourself, or the other person, to another.

*(These preliminaries are outlined in detail in *The Hyperspace Helper: A User Friendly Guide* by Stewart and Janet Swerdlow, Expansions Publishing Company, Inc., © 2004.)

8

The Trinity of Sexuality: Love, Intimacy & Trust

The *Trinity of Sexuality* consists of love, intimacy, and trust. While each of these qualities can be present in every sexual relationship, they can also be mutually exclusive. You can love someone, for example, but not be physically or emotionally intimate with them, or even trust them. Or, you can be physically or emotionally intimate with someone, but not love or trust them. Finally, you can trust someone, and not be physically or emotionally intimate, or love them. Most people with failed sexual relationships have the same issues—fear and lack of trust.

In most modern sexual relationships, whether casual or committed, the desired trinity is rarely complete. The majority of sexual relationships consist of physical intimacy and sometimes even borderline trust, but no real emotional intimacy or love. Most people do not know what love is. In many families, love translates to control, manipulation, and fear—otherwise known as the *Trinity of Mind-Control!* Most people grow up believing that close personal relationships must contain elements of this latter trinity. This type of relationship is "normal" for most people, but dooms a sexual relationship to failure before it even begins.

Most relationships combine the *Trinity of Sexuality* with the *Trinity of Mind-Control* to create a sexogram of Love, Intimacy, Trust, Fear, Control, & Manipulation.

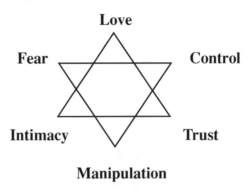

Love is a neutral energy that emanates from the God-Mind and does not discriminate. Because it is not the only energy that exists in God-Mind, contrary to what many people believe, love is **not** always enough.

Many people think that if they simply love their enemies, everything will change. Realize that it is the mind-pattern that attracts the enemy in the first place. Energy must be applied and directed by mind. You can love unconditionally, or you can love someone to death—both concepts use the same energy, but with different applications and implications.

Most people do not truly love all parts of themselves; therefore they cannot love all parts of anyone else. Until you do the release work on the restrictive mind-patterns involving abandonment, low self-worth, and isolation, as well as accompanying mental work to build self-esteem, you cannot truly love yourself in your entirety.

People who do not understand what love really is, find their sexual experiences unfulfilling. Some people equate the number of sexual encounters or the number of people with whom they have sexual encounters, with being loved. In this way they are physically intimate with many people, but without love, these experiences will always be unfulfilling at the deepest levels.

Love is not based in quantity, but quality. Do your release work on your personal issues to learn to love and appreciate yourself, regardless of your past. This is the first step to attract a partner who will do the same. Regardless of where you both are when you meet, at least there are now two willing people working together to achieve a common goal.

There are many layers of love. Unconditional love is the purest and deepest form, manifesting in a pale pink color. This means accepting all aspects of your partner on all levels, which in turn, of course means accepting all aspects of yourself on all levels.

Keep this acronym in mind:

LOVE = Letting Oversoul Verify Existence

This means that you also allow and accept the unconditional love of your Oversoul and God-Mind on all levels, in all your existences.

Intimacy is a word that is misunderstood as much as love. Most males define this word as "sex." However, you can be emotionally intimate with your best friend, or even a parent, without having a sexual relationship with them.

Most females interpret this word as "emotionally connected." Most women want an emotional relationship before they can consider a sexual expression of it. When a woman says she wants to be intimate, she means that first she wants to share her deepest feelings and desires. For a man, this means taking off his clothes and touching each other until orgasm occurs.

Sexual intimacy is more than just a physical relationship. As with all things, correct sexual intimacy begins on the mental level, moves into an emotional aspect, and finally is outpictured physically.

A man runs through this flow quite rapidly. Operating from a survival mode, the male feels a need to get to the point as quickly as possible—since he never knows when an enemy will come along and kill him while he is having sex! The survival goal is to deposit the sperm to as many females as possible, resulting in pregnancy and a wider gene pool, and continue hunting. The ultimate prize is the incredible sensation of orgasm and release. Mentally, this makes the male feel God-like; emotionally, this feeds his ego.

A woman feels the need to take her time. She is in no hurry. Orgasm is not really her goal, rather she longs for feelings of closeness and attachment with someone meaningful. In fact, most women would rather live without sexual activity if there is no one with whom she feels she can be emotionally and mentally intimate. Most women prefer commitment to one male rather than to be sexually active with many.

In general, mental, emotional, and physical intimacy are all tied together for the female. From a survival mode, this is part of the "nesting" instinct—the female wants to know the identity of the father of her children, and she wants to be able to create a home and family life.

Intimacy really begins with a mental connection—it is a mind-to-mind communication. You can be intimate with a person thousands of miles away from you. There is no touching, speaking, or activity necessary—just a state of being and knowing, one to another.

Only after a state of true mental and emotional intimacy is achieved should physical intimacy, or a sexual union, be entered into. True intimacy when achieved on a mental, emotional, and physical level, allows for a cosmic dance that reaches the crescendo of explosive creation between two people—one to provide the energy, the other to nurture that energy into being.

Trust is important for a relationship to survive. Not trusting another person is simply the outpicturing of your inner lack of self-trust.

There are many different kinds of trust. Most people only trust on the surface level. For example, you may trust your neighbor to look after your home while you are away, but not trust him enough to tell him your financial details, much less your innermost secrets and desires.

Allowing yourself to trust makes you vulnerable and open to be hurt. Your natural inclination is to consciously avoid anything that makes you feel pain on any level. Self-sabotage mind-patterns often guide you to trust incorrect people who, right on cue, hurt you! So, when the correct people come along, you shield yourself and do everything you can to *not* trust so that you cannot be hurt once again! It is easy to get caught up in this vicious self-perpetuating cycle.

THE TRINITY OF SEXUALITY: LOVE, INTIMIACY, & TRUST

Most people develop a trust relationship over a period of time. They share a little, then wait to see if they will be hurt. Then a little more, and wait. Sometimes people hurt you without realizing it. If you are in a committed relationship, you will both be willing to work through these miscommunications.

Sometimes people hurt you knowingly, even in committed relationships. The question then becomes—to what are you each *really* committed? What *are* the hidden personal agendas? Can each person deal with his/her own issues and then come together to create a positive, forward moving relationship together?

These are all complex issues. Always keep in mind that each person only reflects the other. The bottom line question is always—with whom do you choose to work out your own personal issues of trust?

When a male does not trust his partner to be sexually faithful, it is because he knows what he would do if sexual opportunities presented themselves to him. In general, statistics show that over 80% of men are unfaithful to their spouses, with 25% of women unfaithful. Statistics can be misleading. It may be more appropriate to say that men exaggerate their sexual escapades to feel more "masculine," while women do not want to admit their infidelities. Realistically, male infidelity is closer to 60% while female infidelity is closer to 50%. This means that there are a lot of people who cannot be trusted, and who are unhappy and sexually unfulfilled.

When you are in a committed relationship that involves sexuality, trust is paramount. Both parties must know that the other person is untouchable by any other. No imprinting should occur to the female by another male, and no energy should be dispersed by the male to another female. That knowing is complete trust. There is no shadow of a doubt by either one. Trust, to be genuine, is also unconditional and implicit.

If you do not trust yourself, then no one else can trust you. Honesty, no matter what the truth, is always acceptable over a falsehood. Always ask your Oversoul permission to speak the truth, and to guide you in speaking the correct words at the correct moment to the correct person. As you increasingly trust your partner, you also increasingly trust yourself.

Fear is a factor in most relationships. Most people fear that their partner will leave them, either willingly or through a health crisis. For this reason, people are always on guard, waiting for the moment when something terrible happens to destroy their perceived happiness. People also fear that their partner will find them physically unattractive and undesirable, as well as mentally and emotionally lacking. Because fear feeds itself, small fears often grow out of proportion, causing people to act irrationally and from an unbalanced, and unhealthy, mental and emotional perspective. Once fear takes root in a relationship, the next step is to do something about it. This usually happens in a negative way.

Control is the first method fearful people try. People think that if they control someone, they can force a relationship. These are desperate people who would rather have something than nothing, even if that something is not that great. They forget that by holding onto something that is incorrect, they keep something that is correct away from them. Rather than liberate and enhance a relationship, control achieves the opposite – it restricts and suffocates. If you must use control to hold onto your relationship, then you need to question why you want this relationship in the first place.

Where is your own self-worth and self-esteem? Is your opinion of yourself so low that the only way you think that you can get someone to love you is by controlling them? If you try to control another, this is because you have some part of yourself that you feel is out of control. Rather than work on yourself and your own issues, which probably are painful, you choose to work on someone else. This only puts your relationship in a vicious circle with no way off.

Manipulation is the next step after control. Many manipulators do not even consciously realize that they are manipulators. Most manipulators are able to justify in their own minds why they do what they do. Usually, it is for the other person's "own good." They may try to manipulate you through setting up a particular set of circumstances, by their words, and/or even through gifts and money.

Manipulators are always people who feel that this is the only way that they can get others to love them. Of course, feelings given out under these circumstances are not unconditional love, but more likely sympathy, empathy, guilt, and in the case of monetary manipulation, greed. Because the manipulator does not give out unconditional love, nor feel it for him/herself, the manipulator cannot receive it back through these falsely established relationships.

Making the other person afraid of being alone or unsupported is a common feature of a loveless union. When a person does not love another unconditionally, yet wants to be with them, the only method of continuing the relationship is by playing on the fears of the other person. When you do not trust another person, you control their every move so that no one else can get energy to them. You play mental games and make the other person feel "bad" about his/her actions. Effectively, you become a "handler," making decisions for the other person in all capacities. If the object of your desire does not think for him/herself, you think that you have "won".

Fear and control are under the umbrella of manipulation. This is how the dominant partner gets the outcome of any situation to be in his/her favor. The weaker partner is always manipulated into actions and emotions that the dominant partner needs to feel secure. This false power eventually crumbles.

People who manipulate usually have abuse issues from childhood that made them feel used and controlled. This obviously brings up fear for your life. Such people compensate for their fears in life by manipulating whatever and whomever they can. This gives them a sense of empowerment which then provides a feeling of security.

This carries forward into their sexual relationships. These types of people tend to force their partners into telling them that they love them, create needs for their partners that only they can fill, and destroy their partners other relationships so that only they can fill the empty emotional void. In short, they make themselves indispensable to their sexual partner, retaining complete control and manipulation of their partner's life. Sooner or later, the victimized partner withdraws or realizes what is happening. This kind of relationship always ends miserably for both people.

Sexually, manipulative people do not make good partners. They tend to be selfish and inconsiderate. They tell *you* what do to for them as well as for yourself. Choice is not an option, even if you are manipulated into thinking that you have choice. Freedom of expression does not occur. The sexual acts are orchestrated and staged so that they "look good," but do not feel good on all levels. Both partners know that something is missing, whether there is acknowledgment or not.

Love, intimacy, and trust are mutually exclusive. Fear, control, and manipulation *can* be mutually exclusive, however they are usually all simultaneously present to some degree, intricately locked in a deadly mind-control trinity.

Sexual relationships are about intimacy, love, and trust. A correct sexual relationship strives to bring these attributes into balance. If you must manipulate and control another out of fear, then the relationship will never be able to get into the deepest levels. If you do not want someone to treat you this way, do not treat others this way. Everyone is afraid at one time or another. Do not judge yourself for this. Release what you no longer need so that something bigger and better can come into your life, in a way that brings you total and complete fulfillment on all levels.

9

Creating Sexual Archetypes

The sexual act, when used properly, is a physical play of hyperspace sentences that create a formula for manifestation and creation. Sexual intercourse is truly a body dance that re-enacts the thoughts of God-Mind during the creative process of the universes.

As you observe the various archetype symbols and their meaning, along with some basic positions, you learn to derive your own sexual sentences to accomplish whatever you wish. Keep in mind that it is the actual thought at the moment of orgasm that is more important than the specific position. The position is merely an enhancement of the thought.

All sexual acts have meaning; nothing is an accident. If you do not consciously create your hyperspace sentence or command during sexual activity, then the positions and acts of the encounter automatically determine this for you. Sex is extremely meaningful and can never be "casual," regardless of society's definition of the phrase "casual sex." This is why during ritual sex, that certain positions are necessary to achieve particular manifestations and goals.

Sexual intercourse is like driving – it may seem automatic after a while, but there is a specific technical aspect and an end result, even if you do not realize it at the moment. Sex, like driving, can be dangerous, if you do not understand it. This is one reason why it is important to be a mature adult before engaging in this activity.

In sexual encounters, positions and actions are extremely important. Kissing, for example, is a throwback to single-cell times when DNA materials were exchanged by one cell injecting DNA into another by simply brushing up against it. Kissing re-enacts this by mouth-to-mouth fluid exchange. The tongue is symbolic of the lower level proboscis that injected material outside of the animal/insect cell, and also used for feeding.

When a male sucks on the nipples of a female, he is requesting nurturing energies to make him feel more physically secure. When a male's nipples are sucked, it means that he is giving emotional and spiritual nurturing.

Semen is a rejuvenator of all body tissues and enhances psychic abilities. Swallowing semen has layers of symbolism and results. Physically, this is an imprinting of energy to be absorbed. This can be a programming issue as well as a need to energize the physical system. Swallowing semen can also be a statement of dominance, and is often done in Illuminati ritual.

When fellatio is performed, there is a need to absorb creative power and rise above a situation in the mind. When cunnilingus is performed, there is a need to prepare the physical life for a new manifestation. The "69" position is an overall statement of the balance between the physical and the nonphysical. While with this position there is no possibility of creation, there is a merging and balancing of energies.

When the female is under the male during intercourse, there is a symbolic replay of the dominion of the God-Mind over the physical realities. When the male wraps his arms and legs around the female underneath him it symbolizes his need to envelop physical reality and control all in front of him. The female wants to be wrapped completely in spiritual and creative matters that will spark something creative deep inside of her.

When the male is under the female, it means that the female needs to be uplifted by the spiritual side only for the sake of helping physical reality, but not for creating anything within it.

When intercourse is performed with the female's legs on the shoulders of the male, it means that he is supporting her future burdens in life and wants to deeply be part of her. The female seeks to relinquish control of her own future to the God-Mind within.

When the male enters the female vaginally from behind her, this represents entering the creative force "into the bottom" layers of physical reality so that the manifestation can grow upward from there. This also indicates using the past as a foundation upon which to build the future.

Anyone who receives anal intercourse feels a need for punishment and abuse. This represents an attempt to create something from the past or a dead issue. Anyone who gives anal intercourse feels a need to punish and abuse others. Anal intercourse can also be a re-enactment of childhood sexual abuse. Those who participate in such activities may have ritual programming mind-patterns.

Experiment with the hyperspace archetypes presented in the *Appendices* to see how you can make them work for you. For example, if a male wants to lengthen the time of his erection, he can visualize the archetype for "Erect Penis" in medium red in the root chakra area. If a male has a tendency toward premature ejaculation, he may want to use the "Ejaculation" archetype with a "Brown X" through it.

If a female wants to achieve or strengthen her orgasm, she may want to visualize the archetype for "Female Orgasm" in the root chakra. If she wants to prevent a pregnancy, she may choose to use the "Pregnancy" archetype with a "Brown X" through it in her uterus.

Read through the archetypes to see how you might use them to enhance your sexuality. In addition, think about the body archetypes that you create during sexual activity, and the ones that you would like to create. Then, create your own archetypes, allowing your Oversoul to interpret them for you. Keep in mind that the archetypes in the *Appendices* are only the most common archetypes and energetic formats. Colors are notated where appropriate. Enjoy the exploration of hyperspace sexual archetypes and sentences as another way to explore the creative force within.

10

Getting On Sexual Frequency

Everything in creation has a unique vibration. A frequency is a rate of vibration that distinguishes one flow of energy from all other flows. There are infinite frequencies within the God-Mind that break down into infinite vibrations. No two things, places, or individuals can have the same, exact identical frequency, because then there would be no separation – the two would be as One.

Because all creation emanates from the Mind of God, underlying each individual frequency is a common frequency that sustains all creation. This explains why all DNA is 97% identical with only 3% differentiating species and individuals within that species.

When similar vibrations band together, a group-mind is formed. When similar frequencies band together, a species-mind is formed. Each species-mind/frequency is unique and all individuals who are under the umbrella of that species-mind/frequency have similar qualities, behaviors, and mind-patterns. The highest frequencies have more diverse and individual mind-patterns. The lower frequencies have more "hive-like" and group-minded individuals.

Animals and insects have a species-mind that is group-oriented. This means that the species-mind thinks as an individual for all of its members. There are no separate personalities under these conditions. Plants have a species-mind as well which is sometimes referred to as a "deva" or "nature spirit."

Since all species-minds are related, each can tap into the others due to the commonality of the underlying hyperspace God-Mind within all of them. This is called "getting on frequency."

When you "get on the frequency" of a species-mind that is not your own, you can assume the traits and characteristics of that species when you are tapped into it. Tapping into a species-mind often and for long durations of time can create DNA to match that frequency. Some individuals, for example, ancient Shamans, can shapeshift into the creatures of a frequency into which they have tapped for many decades. This takes an extremely well-balanced individual who can shift into the frequency and not get lost there without the ability to return.

Ancient hunters used to tap into the species-mind of their prey to make hunting easier as well as to honor the life force that sustained their own. Ceremonies were performed to mimic these creatures to bring the frequency closer.

Why, then, would a human want to tap into another species-mind during sexual activity for a beneficial reason? There are many reasons. When you reach orgasm, for example, the thought held in your mind at that moment is projected out and amplified into creation. Tapping into a species-mind and holding its archetype at the pineal gland during sexual activity enhances this projected thought-form, amplifying the speed and intensity with which it manifests in physical reality.

Bear Frequency

This energy is recommended more for males than females because of the body changes that usually accompany this frequency. Over time, the body becomes hairier and thicker, hands and feet enlarge, and appetite becomes ravenous, often craving dense protein. Male genitalia enlarge and the voice deepens. There may even be an increase in height. The body may prefer extreme cold and want lots of privacy, replicating the frequencies need to go into a cave. The bear energy that you access makes the individual more protective of his partner, often increasing jealousy.

Sex becomes incredible due to its intensity. The *Bear Frequency* causes extremely deep penetration and long staying power. Both partners need to rest afterward, so only use the Bear Frequency when you have time to sleep and refresh yourself. One side-effect is that there is a psychological need for many partners. This obviously does not work in a committed relationship, so use this frequency sparingly if you are married or engaged.

On a mental level, the *Bear Frequency* helps the user reach deep within the mind to retrieve information needed for use in the physical world. This causes deep reflection and contemplation so that correct decisions are made in a timely fashion. Heavy use can also cause the personality to be argumentative. Going deep within the mind to find your solutions makes you feel right all of the time. This is a good frequency for law enforcement and military personnel, as well as politicians.

Dolphin Frequency

The *Dolphin Frequency* is unique because it is not an animal species-mind per se. The brain capacity of a dolphin is actually larger than that of a human. This means that dolphins are more intelligent than humans and also higher up on the evolutionary scale.

As with the energies of all species, dolphin energy exists on many different levels simultaneously. This means that there are both physical and nonphysical aspects to the frequency.

Holding the *Dolphin Frequency* archetype at the pineal gland in royal blue during the sex act causes an automatic shifting of the energies to a hyperspace level in such a way that you feel totally like a non-physical energy and completely protected. This enhances the thought-form as it is projected at the moment of orgasm.

Physically, more body fluids are produced. The body feels more streamlined and easily moves through sexual positions. Using this frequency increases the likelihood of pregnancy. With this frequency, the time of the sexual act is shortened, while the spiritual feelings last for a very long time. The *Dolphin Frequency* enhances a strong mental and emotional connection between the partners to such a degree that they can even know what the other thinks and feels. A closer family bond is created, as well as a deep sense of peace and understanding.

Lion Frequency

The *Lion Frequency* is the highest frequency that can possibly fit into physical reality. In its purest form, which takes on the appearance of a golden winged lion, there is a direct awareness of God-Mind and power. This frequency, unlike all of the others, is used at the crown chakra since it fits at the highest point of the body. The *Lion Frequency* gives the soul-personality a feeling of power, strength, all-knowingness, wisdom, and the ability to blend into All That Is.

Physically, using the frequency enlarges the genitalia and allows for multiple, powerful orgasms. The body becomes hairier with larger shoulders and shoulder blades, with a narrower waist. You move faster, crave proteins, and prefer cool shade, although like warm weather.

Males start comparing their bodies and strength to other men. Both male and females feel a greater affinity with nature and an even greater affinity with cats, desiring to have a lot of space around them. You may feel the sensation of wings on your shoulder blades and may find that you do not speak much, but when you do, it is powerful and meaningful. Orgasms will almost force you to roar!

The female on this frequency wants to be with like-minded females, while the male prefers to be alone most of the time. The male and female both become very fertile but the male will not really want to participate in rearing the children. Both want frequent sex, and at the moment of orgasm may have the desire to roar. Whatever is projected out while on this frequency will be amazingly enhanced and perfect. You will amaze yourself!

Scorpion Frequency

Scorpion Frequency is an unusual energy that is not advised for couples who are committed to each other. In fact, there is a lot of this energy programmed into both male and female Monarch sex slaves. This frequency promotes hostility, aggression, assassination, suicide, pain, and hurt. Not a lovely combination for a relationship!

Scorpion Frequency is centered at the root chakra and has connections to the reptilian brain stem, as do most insect frequencies. This frequency is designed to use sex as a means for survival. Many male prostitutes unknowingly use this frequency to survive in the streets. There is a lot of trickery and deception with this frequency. This is why it is used so much in ritual. People on this frequency masturbate a lot since they cannot enjoy sexual activity with others. To them, sex is more a chore than any type of enjoyment.

Scorpion Frequency creates a heightened sexuality and the need for many orgasms. This frequency is cold and uncaring. However, because the frequency is grounded in Earth-based energy, it enables physical manifestations to appear quite rapidly.

Scorpion Frequency tends to cause anorexia, yet it has amazing strength both physically and nonphysically. A good frequency to use when in physical fight mode, it activates the left-brain as well as reptilian mind-patterns.

Wolf Frequency

Wolf Frequency is closely associated with clan and family, enhancing the development of close family relationships, good times between people or groups of people, and camaraderie.

Wolf energy is warm and nurturing, with an aggressive side that is only excited during family crises or attacks by others. Then, the person on this frequency finds strong support and aid from those around him/her.

The physical qualities of this frequency include a slim figure with lovely hair and lots of energy. The person prefers cooler weather and includes a wide mix of plants and animal proteins in his/her diet. The individual leads a more controlled and regimented life with an occasional wild time.

This frequency is generally extremely loving and caring toward others. Couples who use this sexually are devoted to one another and enjoy life together. *Wolf Frequency* also helps people to understand hard times and dark energies. Using it enables you to get yourself out of many predicaments and challenging life situations in an efficient manner. Child rearing is also made easier for those who use this frequency.

Wolf Frequency maintains a very conventional sexuality that does not go to extremes. However, the frequency is reliable, always promoting satisfaction between the couple. A sense of loyalty and respect pervades the sexual union and relationship. *Wolf Frequency* supports anyone who has been sexually abused or who has a fear of sex, helping him/her overcome these types of issues.

Other Frequencies

You can use these frequencies, or you can explore others to see which ones are the best for whatever your desired goals might be. Everything that exists has a frequency, so the possibilities are limitless.

11

Pregnancy/Birth-Control

When two energies come together and merge with each other, a third, new energy is created. This is why the equilateral triangle and the number three are symbols of creation and perfection. This is also why a male and female unite physically to bring forth a new body for creation.

To promote pregnancy and prepare the female's body to conceive and the male's body to produce the most optimum sperm, both partners need to eat sufficient animal proteins, drink distilled water, and take sea salt baths for cleansing. The male can rub castor oil on his scrotum to induce the testicles to make new sperm. The female can rub castor oil over the uterine area to promote a healthy environment within. She also needs to maintain her calcium and Vitamin D intake to maintain sufficient bone density and support a growing and heavy abdominal cavity. The female should check her progesterone level to make sure that it is normal, as well as her estrogen level to make sure that it is not too high to prevent a pregnancy.

When you decide to have sexual intercourse specifically for the purpose of pregnancy, discuss with your partner the type of child that you would like to conceive. Before you begin your sexual activity, both of you can mentally place a pale orange pregnancy archetype in the female's womb to promote pregnancy. At the moment of orgasm, each of you can then project out a thought-form of this child. End your thought-form projection in brown to ground and anchor it to the Earth. After intercourse, keep the pale orange archetype in the female's womb to sustain the pregnancy.

Ultimately, it is the entering soul-personality that causes the union of the sperm and egg to create a baby. The mind-pattern of that soul-personality cause the DNA to form out of the union of the sperm and egg, becoming the blueprint for the body that is developed for the current lifeline.

The mind-patterns of the mother and father, along with their particular DNA structures, are what attract the unborn soul-personality to them as parents. The new body always accurately reflects the mind-patterns of the soul-personality that creates and enters it. Because the parents can only attract a soul-personality that reflects them, the DNA structure is in harmony with the mind-patterns of all three soul-personalities involved.

When a soul-personality chooses its parents, it is like knowing the type of vehicle you need with the options you want in it. You go to the dealers that have that range of possibilities and order the specifications of what you want. Sometimes the new vehicle does not match what you expected and so you do not accept the order.

In human babies, this results in Sudden Infant Death Syndrome, commonly referred to as "SIDS." This is a fancy term for "we don't know why the baby died." In fact, the soul-personality leaves the body on purpose because it is not content with what it found, or perhaps it completed everything that it could from the situation, so it leaves.

It is not advisable for pregnant women to lift heavy objects, bend too far to any side, or have sexual intercourse past the first trimester, as these activities can cause spontaneous abortions or miscarriages. Some women have a weak cervix and cannot take any additional stress to the area. What is generally accepted in medical terms may not be specifically acceptable to you.

Orgasm past the first trimester can cause premature labor to a weakened cervix, resulting in the loss of the cervical plug. Stimulation of the breasts and nipples can also cause uterine contractions and dislodge a potentially viable pregnancy.

The second and third trimesters of a pregnancy are the perfect time for the woman to learn how to appreciate herself as a person, and not just as a sexual object. This is also the perfect time for the man to learn how to control his sexual desires, and perhaps even learn how to masturbate. During this time of a pregnancy some males have a tendency to stray from their mates. He may find the swollen pregnant body unattractive, he may be afraid that he will injure his partner or the baby, or he may have unresolved mother issues – and he certainly does not want to have sex with his mother! Women may feel unattractive as the body changes, and emotional due hormonal surges.

Women may rub aloe on the expanding abdomen to prevent stretch marks. Use castor oil only after the pregnancy is over, as castor oil can induce heavy Braxton-Hicks contractions in the last trimester.

Sexual intercourse can resume just before the due date since there is an enzyme in sperm that helps dissolve the cervical plug and facilitate dilation. The rhythmic thrusts of intercourse can easily trigger contractions to bring on labor toward the last days. Expecting couples may want to take advantage of this time to physically bond, as it is usually six to eight weeks after birth until sexual intercourse is safe to resume. Even then, with a new baby's unpredictable schedule, some couples are too exhausted to think of anything but sleep.

Do your best to find some private time for yourselves, and help each other with the new responsibilities of parenting. If you are too tired for sexual intercourse, then consider giving each other back rubs, or simply holding one another in bed at night can be quite loving and comforting.

The sexiest thing any couple can do is to produce a baby. Creating something that is the perfect synthesis of the two of you is the greatest feeling and wonder that can be imagined. Look at what your bodies produced!

For couples who cannot conceive there is always the choice of adoption. The soul-personality's true connection is via the Oversoul level, not the physical body. If you decide to adopt, you can still use Sexual Magick Ritual to bring the correct child to you. There are also fertility techniques that can be applied to infertile couples no matter what age. There are many options available regardless of your choice. Never give up and never be disappointed, if your goal is to bring a child into your life.

Sometimes, physical parents are only a means to an end for a soul-personality. The parents' bodies are merely the instruments that create a body for a soul-personality to use. Once a child is in your life, do your best never to control or manipulate him/her. Children do not belong to you – they belong to themselves. Your job as a parent is to guide, care, and love. Then they are on their own. If they want your guidance and care, they will ask you. However, love them unconditionally and let them know that you are always there for them, no matter what.

Some people may decide that a child in this lifeline is not appropriate. If both partners decide in advance of sexual intercourse that they do not wish to conceive, then both can mentally place the pale orange pregnancy archetype with a large, "Brown X" on the archetype in the woman's womb.

If you make this decision, then do not let others change your mind. Having a child to please others only harms and damages the parents and child. This decision highly personal and is really only between you, your Oversoul, and God-Mind.

12

Sexual Magick Rituals

Sexual Magick Rituals have nothing to do with pleasure or procreation in the traditional sense. Instead, Sexual Magick Rituals are used as the process which brings forth a specific manifestation into this reality for a specific purpose. Used in this way, the male and female bodies are really only instruments through which the creative force is channeled to accomplish a predetermined goal. Sexual Magick Rituals are quite serious, and not to be taken lightly.

As you already know, at the moment of orgasm the thought-form that is projected out with the energy of the orgasm is what gets cycled into physical reality. This reenacts the release from God-Mind during the Original Act of Creation. In Sexual Magick Rituals, the female body is used as a step-up transformer of the energies related to the thought-form so that the thought-form can anchor into physical reality. The male body is the electrical charge, or initiator, of the thought-form being projected. This is similar to sperm released to fertilize an egg so that ultimately, a baby (or something new) is brought forth into this reality.

Sexual Magick Rituals are extremely intense and powerful, deriving their origins from ancient rites from other worlds. In ancient times, especially in the original Lyraean civilization, Sexual Magick Rituals were performed to create certain conditions on the home planets such as weather control, improved food sources, peace between two opposing parties, beautification and upliftment of the environment, etc.

Orgies, made famous by the Romans and even the ancient Greeks and Egyptians, were really forms of Sexual Magick Rituals with a common theme. For example, if the Romans had an orgy on a feast day for one of their gods, the idea was to energetically connect to and channel the energy of that god or goddess via the orgasmic flow.

The ancient Greeks used many totally male rituals which by today's standards would be considered homosexual orgies. However, the ancient Greeks knew that such activity amplifies spiritual thought-forms since male-to-male orgasm reflects rather than absorbs and grounds. So, such rituals using all males are like sitting in the sun with an aluminum reflector. The Illuminati frequently use this type of ritual.

Sexual Magick Ritual can be performed with all males, all females, or both, depending upon the desired goals. The bottom line in all of it is that the thought-form projected out from the mind of the male at the instant of orgasmic release is then amplified and grounded by the female body so that it manifests on the Earth plane.

Sexual Magick Rituals were not originally used for the purposes of manipulation and control of humanity so that a few could make slaves out of the many. Unfortunately, those in control of True Knowledge on this planet now use Sexual Magick Ritual for the latter purpose.

In Illuminati religion and culture, sexuality is used as it was originally intended, but instead of being used for positive creations, they use it for negative creations. The Illuminati often refer to Sexual Magick Ritual as "ceremony." For the Illuminati, the "baby" is an event, situation, thing, or astral entity that needs to be incorporated into the physical world for whatever reason the Illuminati desire. Sometimes ceremony is designed to create fetuses or infants for consumption of blood and hormones, or to perform a specific function when the child grows older

Ceremony, like programming, is based on the original natural functions and mind-patterns that are already in place. They are then manipulated and changed into something related, but for a different purpose.

There are numerous ceremonies that can be used to host an entity, or to create something on Earth for either the entity or the Illuminati. Sometimes the Illuminati are the "masters" of the ceremony, and sometimes it is the astral entity. In either case, sex is merely the tool or procedure used to accomplish a goal. Ceremony usually involves sound, such as chanting or singing. Some events use animals, plants, and crystals. Torture equipment may be used in ceremonies that require human and/or animal sacrifice.

A common archetype used for group ceremony is the pentagram, or five-pointed star. In this scenario, there is a female on each point of the star with at least one male performing the sex act with her. Each of the males holds the same thought-form in mind as he ejaculates. The goal is for each "team" to reach orgasm at exactly the same moment to simultaneously amplify the energy. This is easily accomplished via the use of drugs and programming.

A variation of this ceremony involves one female stretched out on an altar or performance mat with five males at each of her points. She is positioned in the shape of a five-pointed star, with arms out to the side and legs spread apart. Then, each male would take turns having intercourse and projecting the same thought-form out. After each male has taken his turn and rotated over to make room for the next, the female is made to climax to ground and anchor the energy of that sperm with associated thought-form into the Earth plane.

Another variation involves a six-pointed star. This is a higher level energy projection. In groups, there is a team at each of the six points. If there is only one female, then there are six males with her. The sexual position is maintained so that there is a six-pointed star formed with each copulation.

There are many different variations on all of the above ceremonies. The more people used at one time, the more important and time-sensitive is the thought-form. In all cases, though, ejaculation must be inside the vagina for a physical manifestation to occur. Ejaculation inside of the rectum is used mainly for the entry pathway of a demonic/astral entity. Oral ejaculation is generally used for an enhancement of the female vessel after a vaginal imprinting has occurred.

When only males are used in ceremony, then a physical manifestation is not required. In such cases, the ceremony is for amplification of astral energies and imprinting into a nonphysical realm for the purpose of connecting the Earth plane to some layer of the astral realms. Generally, most ceremonies involve a mix of males and females. However, the exclusively male component is a powerful mind-control tool since that is a nonphysical genre.

There are also ceremonies that involve four males and one female in the shape of a cross or plus sign. This ceremony involves the four elements of the Earth and is used to impose something physical into the Earth plane. For example, this ceremony is used to change weather patterns, affect nature in some way, or even open DNA in a specific species or groups of species. When a particular species in involved, the participants wear headdresses or skins of the targeted species. They may even ingest the species' frequency by eating the species during the ceremony, or have body paintings of them on their own skin.

Sometimes tattoos are used in ceremony because whatever is permanently imprinted on the body causes that frequency to be sustained within the person's own frequency. For example, a tattoo of demonic-looking creatures on the body attracts and connects the person to that specific energy. Tattoos of animals on the body allow that person to easily tap into the frequencies at will. This is convenient during ceremony.

Body piercings are also sometimes used in ceremony. Wherever there is a ring or implant, the energy of the meridian and chakra that contains the piercing is affected. A nipple ring, for example, causes the heart chakra to be more activated, along with any implants located in that area. A penile ring enhances the energy flow to that part of the body, accentuating the orgasmic reactions in ceremony. This is why many Monarch slaves have tattoos and piercings in strategic places.

Hot oil ceremonies are symbolic of the Reptilian love of volcanoes and lava. Hot oil in ceremony represents the energetic connection of hot ejaculated semen to hot spewing magma. The Illuminati just love symbolisms and double meanings.

There are sexual rituals where the males wrestle nude with each other while oiled. The winner then copulates with the waiting female who holds a high position in the ceremony hierarchy. This symbolizes the strongest or most energetic sperm successfully imprinting the step-up transformer. There are many versions of this type of ceremony. One version has the winner urinate on the loser, symbolizing that the loser is now the winner's slave. Another variation has the winner giving anal intercourse to the loser to show hierarchy status. Oral copulation of the loser means that the loser gives his allegiance to the winner.

Female mud wrestling is derived from ceremony. The mud represents the Earth, and the ability to ground and anchor a thought-form. The male sex slave copulates with the female wrestlers in the mud to represent an imprinting on the Earth Mother of a needed manifestation.

These are some of the most common ceremonies. It would take volumes to describe the totality of ceremonies in detail. Suffice it to say that ceremony is based upon true Sexual Magick Ritual. You can create your own Sexual Magick Ritual with your own committed partner for your own specific reasons. When and if you decide to do this, go to the Oversoul level to determine exactly what to do and how to do it. Used correctly, Sexual Magick Ritual is one of the most amazingly powerful tools available, as it is a way of harnessing and anchoring the Original Creative Force of the God-Mind into this reality.

13

Sexual Programming

The primary purpose of sexual programming is to install mind-control methods of control over specific individuals. Programming sessions involve the use of sexuality and the stimulation of the genitals and other sensitive body parts. Therefore, dealing with this matter is highly sensitive for most people.

During sexual programming, the person is brought to a pre-orgasmic state, and then held there for a period of time. This opens up the mind for input and downloading of information. The person is then "closed" by allowing orgasm to occur.

In the ancient days of Egypt and Greece, sexual programming procedures were done manually. Males were tied down to a table or slab. A potion of narcotics was administered as well as tortuous acts on the body until the person was not fully conscious. At that point, the person was manually brought to a pre-orgasmic state so that programming indoctrination could begin. The male's mind was previously fragmented, thus enabling the compartments of the mind to be available.

The instructions, or programming, were entered three separate times. Often, the person lost consciousness, but the pre-orgasmic condition was still sustained. When the individual successfully repeated the programming instructions back to the programmer, all while in a trance, then orgasm was fulfilled to seal in the programming.

For a female, a similar procedure was applied, except that rape and vaginal trauma was repeatedly inflicted upon her. This was a very early form of Monarch Programming. In this way, the programmed female subconsciously associates sex with programming and instruction performance.

If you then create a religion which bans sexual activity and says it is "bad" and against God, you have a society that can only be triggered sexually if the programmer allows or triggers it.

In modern times, narcotics and technology allows much of the programming to occur without direct hands-on stimulation. The individual is strapped to an electronic chair or table. Via computer, he/she is stimulated into the pre-orgasmic condition. The programming is then fed directly into the brain. Next, the brain of the person is given stimulus to think orgasm has occurred so that the instructions are sealed. Even in this method, there is a three-time input. Programming is always inputted three times to ensure that it is accepted on all levels – conscious, subconscious, and superconscious.

In very recent times, all of this is accomplished by direct satellite transmissions and ground antennae. You can go about your normal routine while your brain is downloading programming. A clue that this has occurred is the need for the closure of orgasm.

Ceremony, or Illuminati Sexual Magick Ritual, enhances sexual programming. The actions of ceremony imprint the sexual programming functions of Monarch slaves. Only Monarchs are allowed to be in ceremony for this reason.

Very high-level sexual programmed slaves are also called Dragonflies. These mind-controlled people are used for ceremony incorporating the white-skinned, blue-eyed, winged Reptilians that are the elite of the elite in the Reptilian hierarchy.

Often, implants are placed in strategic parts of the body to facilitate the mind-control. In the male, implants are often placed in the pineal gland, arm pits, behind the nipples, just below the navel, and scrotum. This is called the "Standard Array." There can also be implants in the penis shaft, arms, legs, and anus. They can be in other places in the body, but these are the most common.

The Standard Array in a female includes implants in the same locations, only instead of the scrotum, they are placed in the vaginal walls and uterus. There are usually implants in the breasts and thyroid areas.

All of these implant sites are sexual stimulants and require direct manual or electromagnetic stimulation to activate various functions. Often in males used for breeding, the scrotum implants increase fertility, and are designed to produce a specific type of fetus. In females, womb implants create a certain type of pregnancy, or even limit or block pregnancies.

Another important piece of sexual programming is the desensitizing of programmed people to certain undesirable or distasteful acts. These include sexual acts that the general public finds repugnant or unsanitary, such as anal or oral stimulation/intercourse.

Both male and females have specific programs designed to facilitate their participation in group ritual sex. In some ceremonies, there are rites where the female vagina is considered to be a rose or chalice, sometimes referred to as the "holy cup." A female hosting a demonic astral entity has intercourse with many males who gain energy and union with this entity via copulation. Then, chosen males are allowed to drink out or orally feast on the mix of semen and vaginal fluids in the "holy cup." This is how the entity bestows honor and super powers on the participants. During sexual programming, it is common to force males to ingest the semen of other males, and sometimes even their own, to enforce the desensitization process so that they are imprinted to participate in these types of ceremonies.

Females are also imprinted by being forced to swallow semen, but not for ritualistic purposes. Instead, this "tags" them by their master or owner/handler so that they remain loyal. They are programmed to believe that ingesting semen keeps them young and beautiful.

Females are often programmed to allow the semen of many males to be ejaculated upon them in preparation for ceremony. When males incorporate astral entities in ceremony, their semen is then considered "holy." If they ejaculate this holy semen on the body of the female step-up transformer, it raises her frequency. Then, other males can copulate with her while projecting thought-forms that will be sped up on their way to physical manifestation.

Females may also be programmed to have sex with various animals or alien creatures for specific ceremonies. In the actual ceremony, males wearing the costumes of animals may be brought in, which is more acceptable to the female participant.

The same desensitization is applied with body parts and fluids of all types. Rape and gang rape is a standard programming activity for both males and females. This allows programming to be entered that includes rough sex with many individuals at the same time.

Often, films are shown to children and adults being programmed. Electrodes are applied to lips, nipples, genitals, hands, and feet that are stimulated while the target views specific scenes. This has a dual purpose. First, it imprints upon the target to become sexually excited by the activities being shown, and second, it traumatizes the person to further fragment the personality and allow for the programming to be entered. Sexual programming takes a wide variety of formats. These are some of the most common forms.

Specifically programmed people often have unique sexual desires because they are programmed this way. While one part of the brain may tell the person that their desires are "wrong," "unnatural," or even "totally perverted," another part of the brain automatically and consciously responds to these types of stimuli. Many specifically programmed people act out their sexual programming without being consciously aware of the true motivating force behind their actions. Some people even begin to accept their desires as "natural" for them. Of course, all programming is built upon the natural mind-pattern, so it is important to explore all aspects of your sexuality so you can find out more about whom and what you are.

14

Sexual Deprogramming

There are many methods of deprogramming for specifically programmed people. Generally speaking, because the programming goes in sexually, it must come out sexually. While the deprogramming techniques do not require physical brutality, reliving the mental and emotional traumas are sometimes as devastating as during the input stage. As the programming comes out, the memories that are released from the individual can feel almost overwhelming.

Because sexual programming is entered by sustaining a pre-orgasmic physical state that allows the mind to open for programming, the same condition must be achieved for the deprogramming process to begin.

This information is very ancient and even pre-dates life on this planet. In modern times, Wilhelm Reich, the famous psychiatrist and student of human behavior, developed procedures to accomplish sexual deprogramming. His work is now illegal in the United States and many other countries. Any of his work that is still in print is innocuous and tempered. Only the government is allowed to use his procedures. Anyone functioning as a deprogrammer needs to be aware of this information.

Males

Only a male can deprogram another male. This is because male energies bounce off one another and do not get absorbed. This prevents accidental installation of programming from the deprogrammer to the deprogrammee, and vice versa. This is why all programmers are males, and all sexual deprogrammers should be male.

To activate the programming that is to be removed, the areas that need to be stimulated to create sexual arousal are in the Standard Array areas: at the pineal gland, under each arm, behind each nipple, just below the navel, and in the scrotum.

Technology exists to create sexual arousal in these implanted areas. This requires these implanted areas to be connected to electrodes that deliver pulses to instigate sexual arousal for the deprogramming purposes. Most people do not have access to this type of equipment. If you do, it implies that you are a programmer or a programmer assistant.

Therefore, most people will need to use the manual methods. These techniques have nothing to do with sexual pleasure or gratification. As with Sexual Magick Ritual, the body is merely used as a technical instrument utilized in a specific manner to produce a specific result. This does not imply that you are gay or bisexual, even if you are.

The deprogrammer can sit or stand in front of the totally nude deprogrammee. The programmed male can stand or lie flat on a table or floor. The deprogrammer must use his bare hands, as gloves or other materials affect the energies.

The deprogrammer begins by touching the pineal gland nerve endings at the forehead and bridge of the nose. Then, keeping the fingers of the right hand there, he touches the base of the scrotum near the perineum with his left hand, observing the reactions of the deprogrammee. The deprogrammee verbally states whatever he sees or feels. If at any time the person becomes traumatized and does not wish to continue, the programmed person must immediately mentally place a brown merger at the pineal gland, as well as place his entire body in brown.

The deprogrammer proceeds by moving the fingers across the middle of the scrotum between the two testicles and under the bottom of the penis and up toward the navel. Simultaneously, he brings the other fingers from the pineal area down over the nose and across the lips, down the chin and neck to the clavicle. Soon, the two hands meet at the pit of the chest.

From here, the two hands separate and move to each nipple, circles them, and then moves to each armpit. Pressure is applied at the armpit which activates the implant network. It is important that the deprogrammee not try to inhibit any erections or body sensations that occur.

The deprogrammer repeats this cycle of movements three times in succession. Then because most people have implants beyond the Standard Array locations, the deprogrammer needs to manually stimulate the top of the head by applying slight pressure, the front and back of the neck, down the back to the anus, the arms and hands, and the legs and feet. This is also done three times in succession.

Finally, the deprogrammer stands to the side of the deprogrammee. Starting at the top of the head, he runs a hand down the back and one down the front of the body slowly and simultaneously three times in succession.

At this point, the deprogrammee should be fully aroused and in a trance-like state or close to it. Now, the deprogrammer must concentrate at the main implant sites of the body, specifically the nipples and scrotum.

Here, the deprogrammer cannot be concerned with gentleness or offending the person. This is serious business. The programmed person must go into the session with the full understanding that these are the procedures and that the deprogrammer has complete reign of the body.

Now, the nipples must be pulled, twisted, pinched, and squeezed to activate the implants and programs associated with them. The testicles must be rubbed, lightly pulled, separated, and kneaded. Occasionally the entire scrotum must be held and squeezed—but not to the point of pain.

Occasionally, the penis must be stroked and the base of the erection should be pressed and held. The opening of the penis must also be pressed and the entrance to the penis head held open.

Pressure must also be held on the anal opening and the armpits. At no time should ejaculation be allowed. If the deprogrammee senses this happening, he must tell the deprogrammer who then stops all actions except pressure on the base of the erection. If ejaculation occurs, the session ends.

During this process, the programmed male must mentally observe all images that come into the mind. He verbally guides the deprogrammer to where on the body the sensations and mental images are strongest. He must remember as much detail as possible to record later.

The deprogrammer and the deprogrammee should decide before each session if there are any mental focal points upon which the deprogrammee should concentrate during the session to get specific information. For example, they may choose to concentrate on the monarch butterfly at the pineal, or a dragonfly. They may chose to have the programmed person do the white rabbit or green spiral staircase. There are endless possibilities.

At the end of each session, the male deprogrammee must be ejaculated. This closes off the programming energies and prevents any more downloading from occurring. This closure act may be distasteful to both parties if they are purely heterosexual, but is a necessary part of the procedure.

The male may be taught to do these procedures by himself. This is acceptable. However, it is not as powerful as when performed with him by another male, as this amplifies the body energy as well as recreates the actual programming processes.

If the programmer finds that the male is becoming dependent on these procedures and finds the deprogrammer to be a sexual object, then the sessions must stop. This can happen with male Monarchs who are programmed this way. The relationship between the deprogrammer and the deprogrammee must remain strictly professional at all times.

It is even possible for the deprogrammer to become sexually excited with his male deprogrammee and this means that the deprogrammer himself has deprogramming to accomplish before touching another person in this manner.

If the deprogrammer works with many clients, he must cleanse himself between sessions. This is accomplished with sea salt baths, flushing the body with violet, and drinking distilled water. The deprogrammer must also privately masturbate to release any sexual contamination that he may have picked up in the session.

Females

Deprogramming females is extremely sensitive, bordering upon leaving the deprogrammer open for sexual accusations and legal issues. Therefore, it is only under certain mutually agreeable circumstances that this can be accomplished. Again, only a male can fully physically deprogram a female because of the way the programs are installed.

A female can coach another female through self-deprogramming sessions, but these will not be very deep. It is advisable to teach the female's husband or boyfriend how to physically deprogram unless these males were actively involved with her in rituals.

It has even been suggested that males be specifically trained to deprogram females who have no emotional connection to them and who do this strictly on a professional basis. This can be construed by some as a form of male prostitution, however, the goals and results are vastly different.

Anyone deprogramming females needs to first read the information regarding deprogramming males. The manual stimulations are the same, except that the labia of the vagina are stimulated in place of the scrotum. Also, the clitoris is stroked instead of the penis. The vaginal walls are stimulated as well as the opening to the vagina.

At some point in a female deprogramming session, there must be physical penetration of the vagina by an erect penis which is then held there as the female concentrates on the pineal gland exercises.

There must also be ejaculation inside the vagina so that the sperm can act as an imprinting of male energy to open up programming functions and alters. There must also be oral stimulation of the clitoris with the female lying on her back with legs held open and the male between her legs facing forward.

Bringing the female to successive oral orgasms in this fashion blasts open programming functions, especially for Monarch sex slaves. There is even a level of deprogramming that requires dual penetration by two males into the vagina simultaneously. This activates mirroring programming in the females and twinning programming in the males.

When stimulating the breasts in females during deprogramming sessions, the entire breast, not just the nipples, must be manipulated. Stimulation of the skin over the uterus is also important.

For closure, manual stimulation of the clitoris and vagina must be performed by the male hand until orgasm is achieved. Rules regarding professionalism and sexual associations are applicable for the deprogrammer-to-female relationship with the same regard as given to the deprogrammer-to-male relationship.

Male/Female

Both males and females have common deprogramming sensitivities in certain required acts as the deprogramming gets extremely deep and close to completion. At some point, both male and female require the re-enactment of oral and anal sexual activity, and possibly even group sexual deprogramming in order to remove the traumatic associations with sexual ritual programming performances.

Basically and ultimately, at this deep level, the persons being deprogrammed must actively participate in a group Sexual Magick Ritual where benevolent thought-forms are produced and projected. In this way, the person goes full circle and no longer associates any negativity with Sexual Magick Ritual. Once this is complete, the person is able to remember his/her True Purpose in alignment with the positive purpose of Sexual Magick Ritual as it was originally created in God-Mind. Sexual Magick Ritual for this reason done in this way breaks down and merges all alters into the original whole, intact personality. This aspect gets quite complicated and breaks all known social mores and personal boundaries. Not many ever get this far.

When one considers the combined aspects of sexually programming people along with the sexual aspects of deprogramming, it is easy to see that people who are specifically programmed often have great difficulty maintaining "normal" sexual relationships. Either they are excited and stimulated by "abnormal" sexual activities, or if they attempt to lead a "normal" sexual life, aspects of deprogramming enter into the sexual activity. Memories may be accidentally opened to which the person reacts. There might be trauma, or a shutting down of all sexual functions. Or, the person acts out the programming by being promiscuous.

Sometimes the thought of sexual activity causes adverse physical reactions as some part of the person recalls the sexual trauma associated with it. Sometimes a programmed person is severely punished for having an orgasm, so the mere thought of this can cause intense adverse physical reactions.

Sometimes during sexual activity memories, thoughts, sensations rise to the surface for which the person has no tools with which to deal, and sometimes afterwards, the person may experience shortness of breath, gasping for air, and a myriad of other body sensations. The programmed person is programmed as a sexual instrument—he/she is programmed not to enjoy the process, and if he/she does, or becomes emotionally attached, he/she is punished for this.

Having a sexual relationship with a programmed person is extremely difficult and challenging. However, with understanding committed partners, and a willingness to break through the programming, it is possible to have a deep, mutually-satisfying sexual relationship.

15

Sexual Fantasies

Because sexuality is really the basis of all creation in this reality, your sexual preferences and ideas are a reflection of your foundational thoughts about your entire existence. And, because all creation originates with the God-Mind, this means that your sexual/creative thoughts are actually directly related to the Original Creative Force of the God-Mind Itself. Examining your deepest sexual thoughts, desires, and fantasies helps you to understand your deepest levels.

Many people deny that they have any sexual fantasies. Most people suppress their true thoughts and desires because of societal controls and expectations. Most people judge their thoughts as "good" or "bad" rather than simply observe and label them. If you label a thought "bad" and then suppress it, the thought still exists—it is just buried inside, gathering strength. When the thought finally surfaces, and it will, there is a strong possibility that the thought will take over you. It is better to proactively and objectively label your thoughts without judgment or criticism, and then pass them up to your Oversoul where they belong. Take control of your own thoughts before they take control of you. The more open and honest that you can be regarding your own sexuality, the more you can find out about your own true self.

When you analyze your sexual fantasies, take them apart piece by piece, and look at each and every aspect of the people, places, and things within that fantasy. In this way, you can determine the actual foundational mind-patterns that have created the need in you to incarnate within a physical reality. This process helps you to understand your needs, emotions, and directions since you first entered into a linear physical reality, as well as helps you determine what still needs to be resolved within you.

Sometimes fantasies and fetishes are the result of abuse issues that occurred in this lifeline or perhaps others. Sometimes they are the results of sexual programming, the acting out of ceremony, and/or the programming itself. Sometimes the conscious mind forgets, but the cellular memory has a need to act itself out. If something was done "to you" your body may take over as it acts it out.

There may be a need to act it out by becoming the aggressor and "do to another what was done to you." Or, you may get yourself in situations where you act out what was actually done to you. This all has to do with your original sexual imprinting and your need to change or modify it, the same as you would with any mind-pattern imprinting. In this type of scenario, you set up the scene so that you can act it out with the hope that you can finally bring resolution and balance within yourself.

Many females, and some males, fantasize about being raped by one or more males. In their fantasy, they get pleasure out of pain and violence. They often set themselves up for the rape by setting the scenario as an "innocent" victim in a location where he/she should not be. This fantasy implies a victimization mentality. Males symbolically represent the God-Mind within, hence the penetration and the creative force in existence. Such a scenario indicates that the individual feels unloved by God and needs to be forced into a relationship with It. The person thinks that God has abused him/her in some way and that God is using him/her for Its own pleasure. This person feels that he/she has no control over his/her life and needs to be punished.

Sometimes a person having this type of fantasy actually was raped. If the person feels a need to be dominated, he/she may feel emotional pleasure. If the person felt physical pleasure even though there was emotional trauma, he/she may be trying to work through his/her confusion. This is no different than being held down and given a back massage against your will. The result is that the back feels physical pleasure even though there is emotional trauma.

The mind-pattern of a person who fantasizes about being raped associates love with pain, and sex with abuse. The person also has a low self-worth and feels a need to be demoralized and demeaned in order to have a self-identity. Such an individual has had many existences where he/she was victimized by others and felt that God abandoned him/her. The only way to feel reconnected to the God-Mind is to be forcefully penetrated by It and made to feel physical pain as a way of relieving and extricating internal pain.

Someone who fantasizes about raping someone else generally has a mind-pattern of self-hatred most likely originating with the person, quite often the mother, who abused him/her. This could also originate from programming violence. In either case, the person learned to associate sexual activity with violence, short-circuiting the natural impulses and masking the pleasure centers.

This sort of violent sexual act is not due to looking for pleasure, but more of a way of punishing the perpetrator of the abuse. A rape fantasy is often the victim's way of "settling the score." The base mind-pattern for someone who fantasizes about rape has to do with feeling that physical reality has not given him/her what he/she desires, so he/she has to take it using force.

Some people have fantasies related to molesting children. These types of sexual fantasies originate from sexual abuse in childhood, or programming violence. All pedophiles were sexually molested as children. People who do not release their mind-patterns always become what they most abhor. Abused children grow up to become abusers of others. They molest children who remind them of themselves as a youngster. If they fantasize about molesting opposite-sex children, the odds are that they are programmed and re-enacting a childhood sexual ritual. Many of those rituals result with the death of the child, which is why so many of the abducted children are murdered by their abusers. To ensure that fantasy does not become reality, it is especially important that people with rape or child molestation fantasies do extensive release and deprogramming work, in addition to seeking professional help.

Many males fantasize about having sex with more than one female at a time. He may even fantasize about forcing himself on them. Such a male has a low self-worth image and needs to feel empowered by overpowering someone weaker. He may also feel that women in his life have dominated him and he needs to fulfill his need to dominate them. On a deeper level, this fantasy means that he feels that God has overpowered him and he has no control over his own life.

The thought of having sex with more than one woman at a time makes a male feel very masculine, wanted/needed, and empowered. This fantasy may indicate that he does not feel creative in his daily life, so this is a way to bring out his creativeness. This can also be a result of genetic memory when males had more than one wife or partner so that the population could be maintained and increased. This can also be the result of an imprinting of programming/ceremony.

Females or males who fantasize about having sex with many males at once, are attempting to receive as much input from God-Mind as possible. They feel that they are not getting enough attention from God, so they must enact a symbolic imprinting in this way. Again, programming/ceremony imprinting could be a factor.

The more people involved in a sexual fantasy, the more aspects of Self exist that need to be reintegrated. There is also an incredible amount of creative energy that emanates through a group of people who are sexually aroused. People who fantasize about sexually connecting with a group of people have a need to connect as deeply as possible to as much of the Creative Force as possible. In addition, there may be cellular/subconscious memory of Sexual Magick Ritual from other lifelines or from programming/ceremony.

Some people fantasize about being tied up or restrained while sex is forced upon them. This is known as Masochism. Sexual pleasure in this case is derived from having absolutely no control over what is done to you. Such people feel that God-Mind has completely abandoned them and they are at the mercy of others. Such individuals had childhoods where they were emotionally, physically, and/or sexually abused and could not remove themselves from the torture. They continue to re-enact these times so that they can release the imprinting.

Sadism is the other side of the coin—this is the person who derives sexual pleasure from giving pain. Most people who derive sexual pleasure from giving pain are acting out what was done to them—only now they are the ones in control. For them, it is a way of balancing out their experiences. They, too, feel like they were abandoned by the God-Mind, but now they are in control.

Many female and male fantasies involve large-breasted woman and/or well-endowed males with huge genitalia. Breasts represent nurturing. Those who need to have sex with large-breasted women feel that they need a lot more nurturing from their mothers as well as physical reality in general. Those who need large penises for sex feel that God-Mind is not being adequate with them and they need more creative power in their lives. They feel that their existence is weak and empty, and they need to be filled with powerful creativity. Those who require anal penetration by a large penis feel the need to be severely punished for their lack of creative abilities. Basically, the more violent and demeaning a sexual fantasy, the more detached and angry the person feels about the God-Mind within.

Having the desire to swallow a lot of semen, or have semen all over the body implies a need to be rejuvenated in life. This also implies a need to be imprinted with creative juices to show loyalty to those to whom you report in life, as well as loyalty to God-Mind.

There may be fantasies that involve the use of animals or plants. Here, the symbolism of whatever creature or plant is used determines the underlying mind-pattern. Copulating with a horse, for example, implies the desire to receive a powerful message that can be used in life. Or, these may be programming/ceremony memories the person is mentally re-enacting.

Fantasies that have snakes writhing on and in the body are for the purpose of opening reptilian DNA. This also implies a mind-pattern of thinking that God-Mind's power of creativity is one of fight or flight. Such an individual is limited in creative thought, and only motivated by pressure and fear.

Fetishes are similar to fantasies in symbolic meaning, but usually fetishes are actually acted upon. There are people, for example, who are sexually stimulated by feet. A fantasy would be thinking about this. A fetish means the person actually does this. Looking at their childhood, it is highly likely that this person was once sexually touched by a foot more than once and felt pleasure from it. Because feet represent stepping into the future and the support structure in the future and present, a foot fetish means that the person is not able to exist properly in the present moment and is always thinking in the future. This person finds this concept stimulating and exhilarating, so he/she is totally excited by the future.

Some fetishes involve having a sexual partner urinate on the other. This denotes a person who is excited by anger (being "pissed off" on) and who also feels like an extremely low-level being who needs to physically be someone's toilet to demonstrate his/her subservience. To take this a step deeper, this sort of person feels like God has "pissed" on them and that they are nothing more than a waste receptacle. People with anal and feces fetishes have similar issues.

Some people have a fetish about orgasm and can only climax in a certain position. This is caused by childhood experiences where abuse is evident. Depending on the necessary position determines the God-Mind influence.

Some people have a fetish of dressing in clothing of the opposite gender. These individuals are the usually the result of parental emotional abuse where they were made to dress in opposite sex clothing as children even though they were mentally "normal" in sexual orientation. Usually, the parents wanted a boy but got a girl or vice versa. Lots of proper therapy is needed here.

Transvestites are individuals who are of one gender but prefer to dress in the clothing of the opposite gender. These are basically homosexuals who want to live life as the other gender, but are not willing to surgically complete the process. This should not be mistaken for cross-dressers, who are heterosexuals who get sexual stimulation from wearing the clothing of the opposite sex.

SEXUAL FANTASIES

Sexual dreams are analyzed in the same way as all other dreams. Everything in the dream is primarily symbolic. The sexual symbolism is used by the mind to demonstrate intensity with creative issues, and/or a need to connect with something.

Many people dream that they are sexually involved with people they know, or who they do not know. This has more to do with the energetic interactions with others than about actual sexual activity. If you dream that you are having sex with your boss or co-worker, this means that you feel strongly connected to that person, and want to share more ideas with him/her. If you dream that your boss is raping you, then this means that you feel that he is overbearing and taking advantage of you. The dream has nothing to do with attraction or sexuality.

Some people may actually dream a Sexual Magick Ritual which the conscious mind has blocked out. In this case, the dream state provides a safe place to see what really happened.

As with all things, the more that you know about yourself, the more you know about God-Mind. The more honest you are regarding your own thoughts, feelings, and emotions, the deeper the access into God-Mind. Most people are not openly honest about their sexual fantasies and desires. And those who are often get caught up in the exploration and physical expression of those feelings without delving into the mind-patterns behind the actions. Take time to explore who you are on all levels. You may be amazed at the information that surfaces once you allow yourself to focus on the totality of your entire spectrum of physical reality experience.

16

Group Sexuality

Group sexuality originates in Sexual Magick Ritual – both the natural and programming versions. Anyone who participates in this type of activity in its original sense must be exceptionally balanced and grounded, with the mind-pattern to blend and use the sexual energies of many people correctly and properly. Without this discernment, there can be an overwhelming issue of contamination of personal energy integrity, and an over-imprinting of mind-patterns that can lead to mental and/or physical illnesses.

In Sexual Magick Ritual, the power of group sex is enormous. The challenge is to keep everyone focused on the same thought-form projection. This usually requires the leaders of the Sexual Magick Ritual, the God and Goddess in Illuminati ceremony, to perform the ceremony first with the others following. This maintains the energetic imprinting until it reaches a crescendo of orgasmic release which in turn allows the manifestation to occur in physical reality.

Imagine the power that could be wielded if Sexual Magick Ritual was performed for a beneficial purpose with all participants in harmony with each other! In legitimate Sexual Ritual Magick, there is an even balance of energies, meaning that there are an equal number of males and females. In Illuminati ceremony, there are usually more males than females in order to create a powerful manipulative event or procedure.

Group sex is not advisable for everyone. Such activity brings out issues of abuse, low self-worth, privacy, and personal integrity. Females must be careful that the males involved are not there to fulfill personal fantasies. Males must be careful to monitor their own personal intentions, and not fixate on genitalia size and number of ejaculations possible.

If you participate with a committed partner, you may not be able to deal with watching your partner engage in sexual activity with someone else. This can easily cause mental trauma and relationship issues if both of you are not fully mentally and emotionally prepared, and in agreement. Even with advance agreement, you may feel entirely differently when you actually see the activity take place. In theory, everything you have talked about may sound great, but in practice you may find yourself with something more than you realized.

Some people believe that it is worse for a male to watch his female partner engage in sexual activities with others than for a female to watch her male partner engage in sexual activities with others. This is because on a subconscious level, the male may psychologically believe that the female is his possession/property that he must protect. Additionally, there is an energetic imprint of the female that occurs when sexual intercourse occurs with a male. This energetic imprint is the equivalent of "marking his territory." Once his "territory" is marked, he may have an issue with another male infringing upon what he considers "his." Additionally, the energetic imprint has a lasting effect upon the female which the male will continue to feel on some level for quite some time.

Some people believe the opposite – that it is worse for a female to see her male partner having sex with another female. This is because the woman feels her home and nesting instincts are threatened. She does not like her male partner imprinting another woman and may feel like a part of him is leaving and deserting her. On some level, she feels that this ties him to another woman and takes a part of him away from her, her home, possibly her children, and threatens her emotional ties to him. In addition, if she has any self-worth issues and sees that he enjoys sexual activity with another woman, she may question her own sexual ability to please him. There are myriad of potential issues for both partners to consider. The thrill of the moment may not be worth the pain of a lifetime.

Some people are sexually stimulated by watching their partner have sex with someone else. More males enjoy watching their female partner, than vice versa. This has to do with both low self-worth issues and self-punishment mind-patterns that may be enhanced by programming. Males with multiple partners also find that their energies become scattered and thinned as they spread their imprinting over a wide number of females. These men become physically and mentally weakened, and easily controllable.

Females must be mindful of which males they allow to imprint energy within them. Women with multiple sexual partners have a higher incidence of mental disturbances because of all of the energetic imprints they allow inside of themselves. Their own mind-patterns become masked and infiltrated with the mind-patterns of many males, ultimately resulting in mental instability.

Both males and females who participate in group sexual activities must remember that there are many bisexual people who engage in this as well. In this setting, it is highly likely that someone who considers him/herself heterosexual might be sexually stimulated by the same sex. It is also possible that a same-sex individual might approach a participant for the purposes of sexual activity. One needs to mentally prepare for such a situation.

After participating in group sexual activity, there is often a feeling of being used. When the excitement calms down and the energy dissipated, many group sex participants feel alone and sad. This is particularly true when group members are strangers to one another and the event has a "one-night-stand" feeling. For emotional well-being, it is always best for participants of the group to get to know one another as individuals before anything physical takes place.

For eons of time people have explored group marriages. Most common is one male with many wives. Less common is one female with more than one husband. Polyamory, which really means loving many, is a lifestyle where a group comprised of both males and females develop intimate relationships with each other, including sexual relationships.

On the other hand, it may be emotionally easier and more sexually stimulating to keep the events limited to strangers who are previously checked for illnesses and motives. This keeps the focus on the benevolent thought-form being projected by the group, rather than on any emotional connections that may be formed between individuals or subgroups within the larger group.

Most of the population does not understand, or would be able to handle, group sexuality. Over the centuries, religion, government, and therefore society, have condemned these acts as being ungodly and unsanctified in any committed relationship. This keeps the masses from discovering the real meaning and power in group sexuality. If the masses realized this power, they might create their own agendas and manifestations that would ultimately undermine and perhaps even destroy the ruling factions of the Earth.

Each person and each couple must comfortably decide what is best for them within their own levels of acceptance. Group sexuality has a myriad of implications on as many different levels. However, when you know the true meaning of sexuality and group sexuality, then you can make your decisions in conscious awareness based upon fact. Understanding the true meaning of such things allows you to choose the path best suited to fulfill your own personal needs.

17

Alternative Sexual Identities

Human beings are not 100% male or 100% female. Males are approximately 60% male and 40% female, while females are approximately 60% female and 40% male. This is why zygotes formed at the moment of conception are sexless until several weeks later when the mammalian genetics open, allowing sexual differentiation to occur. This explains why females produce male hormones like testosterone, and males have female hormones like estrogen in their bodies. This also explains why the clitoris is analogous to the penis, the ovaries to the testes, and the nipples in both sexes can emit fluids and are sexually sensitive.

Human beings are hybrids of mammalian and Reptilian DNA. Because the Reptilian donors are androgynous, androgynous genetics are carried within all humans. This androgynous DNA actually pushes humans more toward androgyny than heterosexuality. Many ancient cultures were openly bisexual like the ancient Greeks, Arabs, Mongolians, and many native cultures. Females were used mainly for procreation while recreational sex was mainly same sex.

In modern society, the official prognostication is that over 90% of the population is heterosexual. In fact, these numbers are created because most people are ashamed to say that they have desires for same sex encounters at times. To conform to societal expectations, most people want the official label of "heterosexual," so this is the primary response given when responding to surveys.

Bisexuality does have its place energetically. Male-to-male sex acts as a booster. Females act as a step-up transformer for physical manifestation. This is why they become pregnant and create new physical life. The ancients knew that as a pure ritual ceremony, it was wise to have male-to-male contact as a booster of energy before that actual male-to-female final sexual act. This creates the most powerful transmission of semen and projection of thought-form during orgasmic release. Similarly, female-to-female sexual contact leads to greater absorption of energy before the female-to-male copulation. This is all part of a greater cosmic formula for sexuality within a physical reality.

Bisexuality is balanced and centered in the pineal gland area/ superconscious mind, recognizing that both sexes are equally of God-Mind. God-Mind is not prejudiced by plumbing, and sees the beauty in all body types. Bisexuality is more prone to the pleasure for positive purposes rather than as an ulterior motive. Because programming is built on the most natural functions of humankind, heterosexuality is promoted to hide from humans the true state of their sexuality. Bisexuality is desired for those who have access to True Knowledge. For this reason, bisexuality is easily used in programming and Sexual Magick Ritual ceremony for the Illuminati. Most Monarch sex slaves are bisexual for this reason.

Heterosexuality is based all in the left-brain/conscious mind. Such people tend to be materialistic, egotistical, and self-centered, leading to rape and abuse of self and others, as well as a type of schizophrenia. Homosexuality is centered in the right-brain/sub-conscious without balance, and could also be considered a type of schizophrenia.

Homosexuality occurs for several different reasons. Often it is because the soul-personality has many consecutive linear lifetimes in one gender so has an affinity to a particular sex based on soul-memory. The soul-personality may choose to incarnate in the opposite sex to help create inner balance.

Another reason for homosexuality stems from childhood imprinting of a sexual abuse situation where the person is imprinted with the idea that sexual pleasure can only come from one particular gender. Sometimes the abuse is not sexual, but if it were perpetrated by a male upon a female, the female has such a hatred of males that she decides to live a lesbian lifestyle. Or, if the abuse is perpetrated by a female upon a male, the male has such a hatred of females that he decides to live a gay lifestyle.

Sometimes people perceive themselves unattractive to members of the opposite sex, so they choose a homosexual lifestyle so they do not have to face this issue. Sometimes due to sexual abuse or programming, people really do not know to which sex (or both) they are attracted. Sometimes people have homosexual alters programmed into them for ceremony purposes, and these alters are active in a person's every day life, creating a need for him/her to live as a homosexual.

Homosexuality can be caused when the soul-personality coming into the body changes its mind at the last minute and decides to mentally be the opposite gender of the body that it created within the mother. This might be due to a last minute decision about the specific goals of the soul-personality. Or, a male-skewed soul-personality creates a male body in which to be born but suddenly decides to have a female orientation so is born homosexual.

Homosexuality can also happen when there is a last-minute switch of the soul-personality into the body at the end of pregnancy. A female-oriented soul-personality of the same Oversoul, for example, takes the place of a male-skewed creator of the body for some reason decided upon by the Oversoul. Sometimes, adults opt for sex change operations so that the body matches the orientation of the soul-personality.

Sometimes, the soul-personality of the gender-different body decides to totally experience that body in every way, including sexually. This means that the person works to overcompensate for the body difference. Such males, for example, become aggressive and dominant gays who seek to cause pain, and pleasure through pain, to other males. Such females tend to be completely feminine and submissive to lesbian partners, and are quite often abused by their partners.

Some people are born neither male nor female, but a complex combination of both. In fact, there is an organization called the "Intersex Society of North America" whose motto is "building a world free of shame, secrecy, and unwanted sexual surgeries since 1993." According to their information, these types of births are much more common than most people realize.

This organization says that in approximately one out of every one-hundred births, there is a baby born whose body differs from that of the standard idea of a male or female body. And, according to their statistics, one to two out of every one-thousand of these babies are surgically corrected to fit the conventional standard male/female body type.

When a baby is born, the first question that parents are asked is "Is it a boy or a girl?" What happens when the sex is not immediately determinable? Sometimes it can take days before the medical community can come to a consensus about what the child is and what should be done about it.

The standard procedure is predominantly to "normalize" the genitalia as soon as possible and then treat the child in the same way you would that sex. However, the Intersex Society of North America is lobbying the medical community to observe the emotional and psychological maturation of the child to see with which sex he/she most identifies.

This is an extremely difficult for parents. They must deal with challenging questions and make even more challenging decisions. It is equally important for the parent to look at the mind-patterns of the professionals who guide them through this process—if the professional does not come from a balanced mind-pattern, then how can he/she help the parent make the correct decision for the situation. If the health of the child is not at risk, then is surgery acceptable under any circumstances?

This brings about an even more challenging societal question— should there be a "third sex" – perhaps a category called "androgynous"? After all, God-Mind is without gender. Perhaps these people are a genetically-closer personification of the Original Creative Force? Perhaps they are surgically altered and forced to fit into an "either/or" mind-pattern that makes them more controllable as part of the masses. Perhaps if they were allowed to live as they were born and fully express this mind-pattern, they would be a threat to the powers-that-be?

Are they, perhaps, ahead of the evolutionary process? Are they forerunners of the genetic evolution of humankind? Is the medical community's "standard of care—quick-fix surgery" developed to prevent the rest of the population from seeing a glimpse of their future? Will this status at some point be what others wish to achieve? Will those without a physical representation of androgyny feel "less than"? Are intersex people more "normal" than those people with the accepted male/ female body types?

When you really think about some of these issues, you begin to re-think the term "alternative sexual identities," what it really means, and who the people really are who fit this description. Who knows— perhaps *you* are the one with the alternative sexual identity!

18

Your Sexual Code of Conduct

Most likely, you have within yourself a "sexual code of conduct" that has somehow formulated throughout your years. The original imprinting usually starts with the parents and how they address the physical genitalia. From there, most people have the suppressive teachings of their religions, added to the sexual messages of promiscuity advocated by the outer world, in addition to all the other outside influences that try to break your spirit and turn you into something that you are not.

You internalize this combination of sexual signals and come up with your own personal sexual code of conduct. Once in place, few people revisit their thoughts and feelings. What do you really believe about your own personal sexual nature, and why? Are these your own thoughts and feelings? Or are these thoughts and feelings imposed by others in such a way that you eventually took them for your own?

Some people become quite sexually promiscuous in their rebellion against society's sexual restrictions. Some people have great difficulty engaging in any sexual activity at all. Still, others lead a "middle of the road" sexual lifestyle without extremes one way or the other. Ultimately, all of these groups of people will need to look at what they do and why.

The more honest that you are about your sexual preferences, the more you find out about who and what you are, as well as your personal connection to the God-Mind Itself. Now is the time to go into this part of yourself to determine what part of sexuality intrigues you and why. Look beneath your outer actions to determine the circumstances of life that led you to develop these preferences and desires.

Anything that you see but do not like, release up to your Oversoul. Watch the thoughts move out of your personal space and straight up into your Oversoul. Do not judge or criticize, but simply observe. You are looking at a part of yourself. There is a part of you that likes whatever you see, or it would not exist within your mind-pattern. These can be scary and intimidating thoughts. You may think that if you tell someone else, that will be the end of your friendship or relationship.

Sometimes you may need help in sorting out your sexual code of conduct. You may need to go to a professional who can help guide you through the process. If you choose to do this, go with an open mind. Even though what you need to say may be difficult or even embarrassing, most likely the professional has heard similar stories before.

As with changing any mind-pattern, it can be disturbing when you find out you are not the person that you thought you were. You have to come to terms with your sexual preferences, fantasies, fetishes, and dreams. You may want to label some of these thoughts "bad" so that you can judge and punish yourself. Instead, continue to release everything and find the source of the original imprinting.

You may find out that the original imprinting started in another timeline. Or, it may be from sexual programming. You may uncover sexual memories from your childhood that you have buried. You may have to tell your partner something that you like/do not like that may be uncomfortable for you.

When you get into your sexual side, you often have to face your own inner pains and inner shames. You have to label the origin of these feelings to determine what you want to keep and what you are ready to discard. You may find that you hold onto a sexual code of conduct that no longer fits who and what you are as you continue to explore your own Self.

You may find that you have been silent for too long. Even if you are surrounded by people, it is still possible to be emotionally isolated. This is all about being true to yourself, and releasing all the energy in your auric field that is not yours in the first place. How did you come to be who and what you are? How did you devise your sexual code of conduct? Is it time to revise it?

When you stop judging your own sexual intrigues and interest, and start observing them, you may be amazed what you can finally learn about yourself. Like all other aspects of your soul-personality, your sexual side also needs deep, honest exploration. Even though sexuality is the most publicly exploited subject, the true meaning of sexuality is one of the best hidden secrets. And, where is the best place to hide secrets where no one will find them? Right in front of you! So, be honest and open, and be who you are as you revisit your own sexual code of conduct. You may be fascinated at the new information this deeper level of exploration reveals!

Appendices

Basic Sexual Archetypes

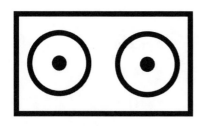

medium green

Breasts
Symbolize empowerment/
nuturing of heart/
emotions/physical reality.

pale orange

Egg

pale orange

Egg, Fertilized

pale orange

Egg, Fertilized in Womb

Ejaculation

bright red

Intercourse

dark red

Orgasm, Female

bright red

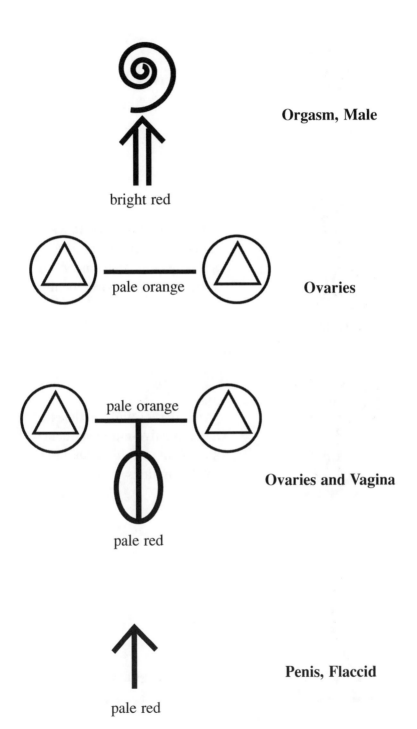

Orgasm, Male

bright red

Ovaries

pale orange

Ovaries and Vagina

pale orange

pale red

Penis, Flaccid

pale red

pale red

Penis, Erect

medium red

Penis, Erect and Testicles
Symbolizes power in new
beginnings to create energy in
spiritual space/environment.

medium red

Penis, Erect and Testicles
Using creative empowerment
of environment to create fast
new beginnings (physically).

pale orange

Pregnancy

Pregnancy Prevention
Pregnancy archetype in pale
orange; "X" in brown.

Semen

silver

gold **Sperm**

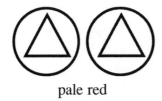

Testicles

pale red

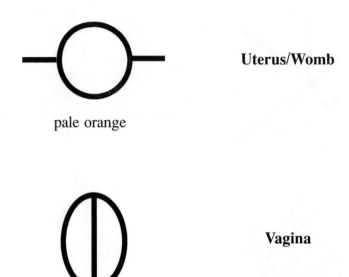

Uterus/Womb

pale orange

Vagina

pale red

Vagina, Open/Penetrated
Symbolizes containing
space within the
context of time.

pale red

Basic Body Shapes Created During Sexual Activity

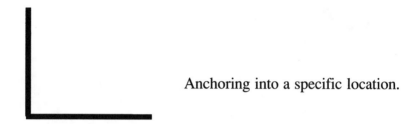

Anchoring into a specific location.

Ending a situation.

Fast power generator.

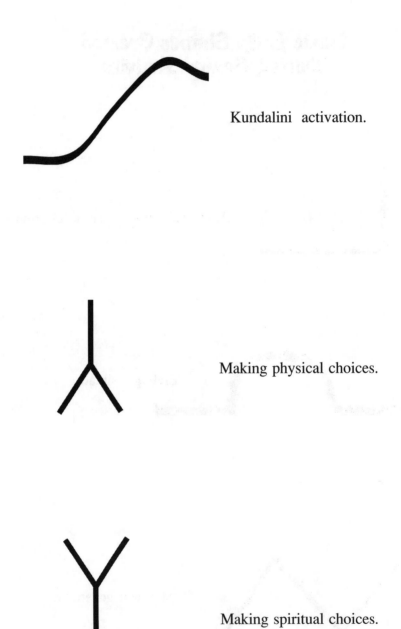

Kundalini activation.

Making physical choices.

Making spiritual choices.

Basic Couples Positions Archetypes

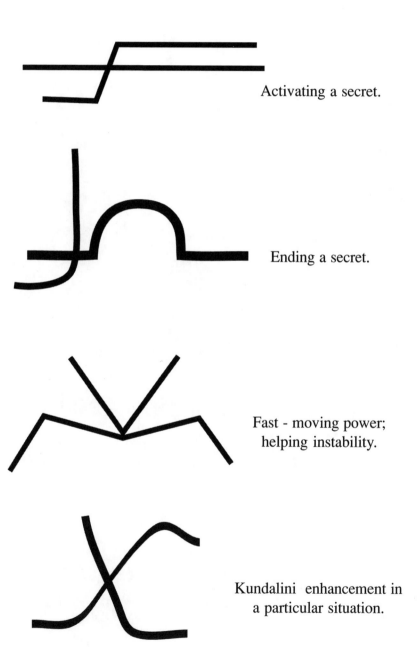

Activating a secret.

Ending a secret.

Fast - moving power; helping instability.

Kundalini enhancement in a particular situation.

Basic Sexual Positions
Archetype Sentences

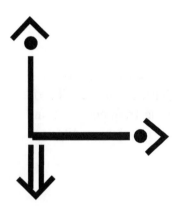

Anal Intercourse
Mind-Pattern of punishment
without a possible physical
reality manifestation.

**Basic Male/Female
Sexual Position**
Manifesting something
spiritual in physical reality.

Connection
Male and female.

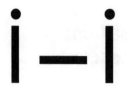

Connection
Union.

Cunnilingus
Causes manipulation of
time frequency within
physical reality.

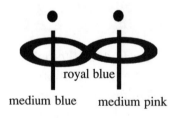

Enveloping
Causes emotional, mental,
and physical union of a high level.

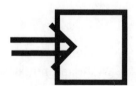

Fellatio
Brings creativity to
physical reality.

Female/Top Position
Keeps creations in astral rather than physical. Causes Earth energies to choose timing of the manifestation.

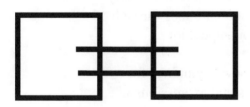

Kissing
Equalizing the expressions of physical reality.

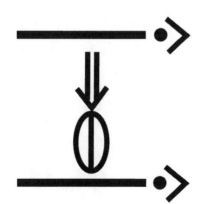

Male/Top Position
Manifesting something physical in physical reality.

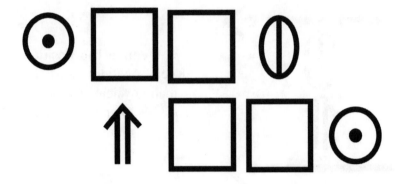

"69"
Creates two DNA sentences.

Becoming aware of physical reality
expressions and emotions through
time manipulations.

Power in new beginnings for
the emotions and expressions of
physical reality to open awareness.

Frequency Archetypes

Bear Frequency
Golden brown at
pineal gland.

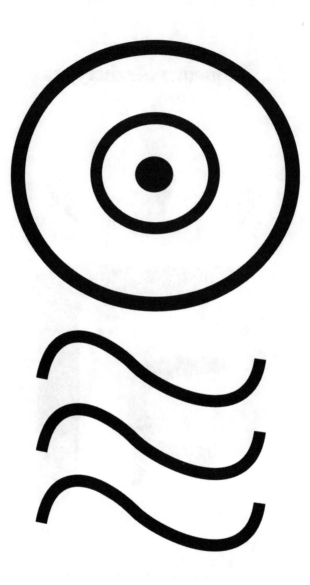

Dolphin Frequency
Royal blue at the
pineal gland.

Lion Frequency
Violet diamond; gold aleph;
royal blue dot at the
crown chakra.

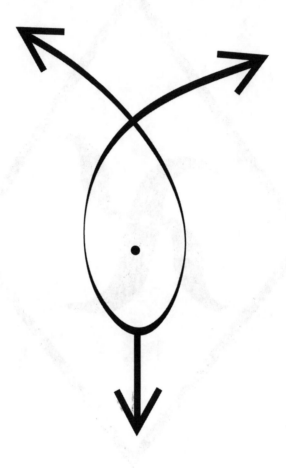

Scorpion Frequency
Brownish-red at the
root chakra.

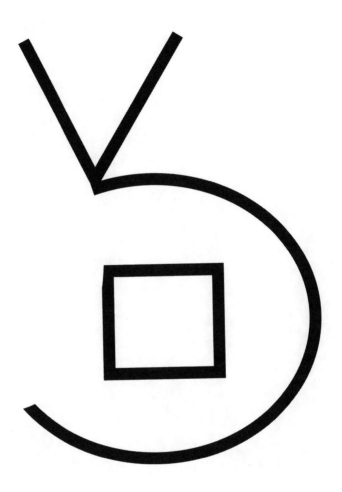

Wolf Frequency
Tan to brown at the
pineal gland.

Sexual Exercises/Visualizations

The following exercises are designed to open and enhance your sexual life. They will help you to more freely explore the sexual side of yourself, which in turn greatly accentuates the creative and spiritual aspects of Self.

The preliminaries* referred to in some of the exercises mean to balance your T-Bar at the pineal gland or center a royal blue dot in a royal blue circle at the pineal gland. Then, do some cleansing breaths in through the nostrils, hold a couple of seconds, and blow slowly out through the mouth.

*(These preliminaries are outlined in detail in *The Hyperspace Helper: A User Friendly Guide* by Stewart and Janet Swerdlow, Expansions Publishing Company, Inc., © 2004.)

Achieving Orgasm

Some men and women are unable, or find it difficult, to reach an orgasmic climax during sexual activity. The mind-pattern that creates this usually comes from childhood sexual abuse trauma where sexual sensations were associated with pain and inappropriate touching by someone else. Sometimes, it comes from sexual programming when sexual orgasmic release was forced upon the person when closing a programming session or via Sexual Magick Ritual ceremony. The other common mind-pattern is found in people whose religious background and indoctrination prohibit them from enjoying any sexual activity because they are taught that sexual intercourse is allowed for procreation purposes only.

The following techniques are designed to help such individuals to achieve the sensation and pleasure of orgasm. Before you begin, you must decide to allow yourself to feel this without guilt or shame. This is a natural process and a God-given right. You can practice this by yourself or with a partner.

For a male:

Move the center of consciousness from the pineal gland area to the genitals at the root chakra after doing the preliminaries. Place the entire body in pale to medium red. Visualize the erect penis archetype at the root chakra. Start by manually stimulating the scrotum and shaft of the penis. Be slow and methodical, with your goal to achieve an erection. Use castor oil or saliva as a lubricant.

Stimulate the nipples by gently stroking, pulling, and twisting. Some men find that stimulating the anus is also sexually exciting. In your mind, replay your deepest sexual fantasy at least three times in a row. In all cases, the fantasy should end with an amazing orgasm.

Concentrate stroking the tip and shaft of the erect penis while holding the erection archetype in mind. Then place the male orgasm archetype in the center of the root/base chakra.

If at any time the penis should go limp or soften, go to brown, balance the T-Bar, and start over. Ultimately, by the third cycle of this exercise, you should have achieved orgasmic release and allow the ejaculation to flow. Do not try to stop the build-up of energy nor should you worry about the ejaculate flow.

For a female:

After the preliminaries, move the center of consciousness down to the root/base chakra and place the entire body in an orange/red color. Visualize the female orgasm archetype in the clitoral area.

Begin to stimulate the labia of the vagina and the inside walls of the vagina, using castor oil or saliva as a lubricant. Go slowly and allow the fingers to gently stroke the clitoris and the nipples of the breast.

Put extra but gentle pressure on the upper walls of the vaginal canal and use the thumb as a pressure point on the clitoral hood. Do not be afraid to orgasm to quickly and allow the energies to flow as they build in the area.

Should you experience any pain or discomfort, stop, ground, and balance before starting over. Concentrate on the female orgasm archetype at the root chakra and hold in the mind your deepest sexual fantasy. Allow the scenario in your mind to end with orgasmic release. Do this three times until you feel yourself reaching orgasmic sensation.

Attracting a Partner

First decide in your mind what type of partner you want to have. Then do the preliminaries.

Centering your consciousness at the pineal gland in royal blue, create a computer screen and keyboard in front of you. This is your own mind, so the computer configuration can look like anything that you wish.

On the screen, create the image of the person with whom you want for a sexual partner. Make the image as perfect and clear as you possibly can. Then, when you are satisfied, place the image on the screen in brown and save the program on the computer. Next, place yourself in brown.

Connecting to a Partner

If you already have a committed sexual partner and want to enhance your connections, after doing the preliminaries visualize the person standing in front of you face-to-face. Then, start connecting yourselves chakra band to chakra band, starting at the root chakra and working up to the crown chakra. Use the appropriate color for each chakra band, i.e., the pale red connection line for the pale red chakra bands, pale orange connection line for the sacral chakra band, etc.

Once all the chakra bands are connected in the corresponding color, envelope both of you in brown. This is the equivalent of a mental, or energetic, tantra exercise. You can even do this together as a sexual encounter prior to sexual intimacy.

Determining Sexual Orientation

There are many individuals who are confused about their true sexuality. This exercise helps you determine your sexual orientation in this reality at this time.

Take a look at your most hidden and deepest sexual fantasy, as this determines your true relationship to the God-Mind and why your life is the way it is. Beyond the symbolism of the people and events, this fantasy also shows you the type of person to which you are most sexually attracted.

Do not be ashamed if you see a same-gender person. Simply observe. If you could have a sexual partner right now without any questions asked, and without anyone ever knowing or caring, who would this be? Is it more than one person? What gender is that person or persons? What do you want to do sexually with this person/these people?

Then ask yourself—could I actually do this in physical life? If your answer is "yes," then go to the Oversoul level to see if the fantasy is appropriate to act out in this reality. If the answer is "no," then ask yourself why not. Is this because of what others would think? Would you be hurting someone by these actions? Are you living a lie?

You also need to look beneath the fantasy to see if any programming is involved. In other words, is this really your fantasy, or is it a programmed memory that is surfacing? You may want to incorporate some deprogramming techniques to make this determination.

No matter what you decide that you are sexually, you must be that. Forcing Self to conform to what others or society claims for you is debilitating. You must be you. You must freely express yourself sexually in a manner that fits who you are; otherwise you will never be your full potential.

Exploring Stored Sexual Cellular Memory

Do the preliminaries. Center your consciousness at the pineal gland in royal blue. Then, slowly start to move the center of consciousness down slowly through the body until you reach the sacral chakra between the navel and pubic bone. Place your consciousness in the pale orange color of that chakra band. Simply observe what comes up. As memories come forward, flush them with violet and send them up through the crown chakra into Oversoul awareness.

Now, slowly move the center of consciousness down into the root, or base, chakra band between the pubic bone and top of the thighs. Again, simply observe what comes to mind, sending any traumatic memories up into the Oversoul as before.

When you finish observing, move the center of consciousness back up to the pineal gland slowly. Place it in royal blue. Then balance your T-Bar and go to brown to ground and balance.

You may want to write down all of the memories that you sent up to your Oversoul so that you can use them later as a focal point for deprogramming techniques, or with the *Green Spiral Staircase* exercise as delineated in *The Hyperspace Helper.* *

---

*(These preliminaries are outlined in detail in *The Hyperspace Helper* by Stewart and Janet Swerdlow, Expansions Publishing Company, Inc., © 2004.)

Premature Ejaculation

Men with premature ejaculation issues have a mind-pattern of low self-worth and self-sabotage that can be corrected with release work. This also involves a fear of creating as well as not wanting to please Self or another person. All of this goes back to parent issues.

Premature ejaculation is only an issue when you have intimate relations with another person. Therefore, while engaged in sexual activity, visualize the erect penis surrounded by pale red, as a base layer, and then place ice blue over that as a covering layer. This should diminish or stop the need to ejaculate until you are ready. See the male orgasm archetype at the erection with a brown "X" through it.

If you feel that you are about to climax, stop all body movement and allow yourself to relax to a pre-sexual condition. It can also help to apply pressure to the base of the penis to reduce blood flow to the erection until the sensation passes. Once the sensation of near orgasm subsides, you can resume sexual activity.

When you are ready to climax, remove the ice blue layer from the erection, intensify the red color, and place the male orgasm archetype over the erect penis. You may need to start and stop several times until you finally allow the ejaculation to occur and then project out a thought-form for physical manifestation at the same time.

After orgasm, it is always helpful to close off the sexual energies by going into a deep brown color. Balancing the T-Bar and/or centering the royal blue dot within the royal blue circle also helps to regulate the sexual energies properly.

Removing Sexual Blocks

Often, both men and women have issues performing certain sexual acts even though their partner may want to participate in them. There are also some people who are completely afraid of any sexual experience with anyone.

To work on removing your sexual blocks, do the preliminaries and stay centered at the pineal gland in royal blue. Then, place the name of the act in brown block letters at the pineal gland and observe what you see. For example, if you have an aversion to fellatio or cunnilingus, place that word at the pineal in brown block letters. The issues or reasons associated with these acts will come into your mind. You may see, or feel, an event, a picture, a word, phrase, or even hyperspace archetypes.

No matter what you see or feel, these are important issues. As you start to work on your issues, the aversions and disgust will abate and/or diminish. Depending upon what you see or feel, you may need to do deprogramming techniques, release work, or visualizations, such as placing a big brown "X" through the images and words.

Work on these issues until you feel you are able to attempt the act or acts. Once you have actually tried them, you can decide whether or not you like them – then you are finally free.

Sexual Affirmations

Accepting Your Body

I accept that my mind-pattern creates my physical body.

I accept my physical body as a product of my personal creation.

I accept my body "as is," without judgment or criticism.

I feed and exercise my physical body correctly.

I love all parts of my physical body.

I use my mind-pattern to uplift and elevate my personal body image.

I allow myself to look at my physical body without guilt.

I allow myself to explore all parts of my physical body without guilt.

My body is magnificently beautiful.

My body constantly regenerates and rejuvenates as needed.

Attracting the Correct Partner

I allow myself to attract the correct partner who meets all my needs.

I now attract the correct partner who meets all my needs.

I now have the correct partner who meets all my needs.

I am worthy of attracting the correct partner who uplifts and supports me in all ways.

I now have the correct partner who uplifts and supports me in all ways.

Connecting to the Creative Force

I am connected to the Creative Force of the God-Mind.

I feel the power of the Creative Force of the God-Mind flowing through me.

The Creative Force of the God-Mind flows freely through every cell of my being.

I am a conduit for the Creative Force of the God-Mind.

I allow the Creative Force of the God-Mind to flow into all areas of my life.

I use the Creative Force of the God-Mind as a step-up transformer for my own creative force.

Connecting to Frequencies

I understand how to connect to the correct frequencies to enhance my sexual activity.

I use the correct archetype and color code to connect to the appropriate frequency.

I consciously connect to the appropriate frequencies as needed.

I explore all frequencies to learn about their appropriate uses.

Fear, Control & Manipulation

I take control of myself so that no one can take control of me.

I release all inner fears to my Oversoul and God-Mind.

I am always in control of myself, in alignment with my Oversoul and God-Mind.

I release the need to control anyone via fear, control, and manipulation.

I forgive myself for trying to control anyone via fear, control, and manipulation.

I release anyone who tries to control me via fear, control and manipulation.

I forgive anyone who tries to control me via fear, control, and manipulation.

Masculine/Feminine Energy

I easily identify any masculine/feminine energy that is out of balance.

I understand the proper expression of masculine energy within this physical reality.

My masculine energy is now appropriately balanced within myself.

I understand the proper expression of feminine energy within this physical reality.

My feminine energy is now appropriately balanced within myself.

My masculine/feminine energies within myself are appropriately balanced in the proper ratios.

Masturbation

I allow myself to look at my own genitalia without guilt.

I allow myself to physically explore my own genitalia without guilt.

I allow myself to touch myself in any way is physically comfortable and pleasurable for me.

I allow myself to masturbate as a way of connecting to the Creative Force.

I connect to the Creative Force via masturbation.

I allow myself to use masturbation as a deprogramming tool.

I sexually deprogram via masturbation.

My masturbation processes are balanced.

Orgasm

I allow myself to easily achieve orgasm.

I allow myself to achieve orgasm through masturbation.

I allow myself to achieve orgasm with a committed partner.

I easily achieve deep and satisfying orgasms.

I connect to the Creative Force of the God-Mind through orgasm.

I easily create physical manifestations through orgasmic release.

I am able to speed up my orgasmic release at will.

I am able to slow down my orgasmic release at will.

Physical Sexual Archetypes

I understand the archetypes that I create during sexual activity.

I understand the archetypes that my partner and I create during sexual activity.

I release all body movements during sexual activity up to my Oversoul and God-Mind for explanation.

I use the archetypes my body creates during sexual activity to aid in the physical manifestation process.

Pregnancy

I release my fear of parenting.

I release and forgive my own parents.

I release my fear of children.

I review, accept, and release my own childhood.

I release anything that blocks my ability to procreate.

I am worthy of creating a physical child in this physical reality.

I deserve to be creative and bring forth a child into this physical reality.

I connect to my Oversoul and God-Mind to know how to be a wonderful parent.

I state my desires and requirements for my child on the inner levels.

I communicate on the inner levels with my not yet conceived child.

I communicate on the inner levels with my unborn child.

Protection from Outside Influences

I release the need to be sexually influenced by outside sources.

I release the need to act upon outside sexual influences.

I maintain pale red in my root chakra regardless of outside influences.

I remain sexually balanced regardless of outside influences.

I release all excess sexual energy up to my Oversoul for safekeeping until the proper time.

I recognize sexual stimulation from ELF bombardments.

I deflect all sexual stimulation from outside sources.

I keep myself in heavy violet to deflect ELF bombardments.

I deflect all undesired outside sexual influences, even while I am sleeping.

Self-esteem

I am worthy of a long-term relationship.

I am likeable and loveable.

I am worth of unconditional love.

I recognize my own talents and abilities.

I appreciate my inner and outer beauty.

I deserve to have a fabulous sexual relationship that fulfills all my emotional and physical needs.

Sexual Code of Conduct

I identify my personal sexual code of conduct.

I explore my personal sexual code of conduct without judgment or criticism.

I identify the origins of my sexual code of conduct.

I explore the origins of my sexual code of conduct without judgment or criticism.

I accept my personal sexual code of conduct without judgment or criticism.

I easily determine any necessary changes within my sexual code of conduct.

I easily release all unnecessary parts of my old sexual code of conduct.

I change my sexual code of conduct to match my current belief system.

My sexual code of conduct now matches my current belief system.

Sexual Fantasies

I stop hiding from my own sexual fantasies.

I acknowledge all my sexual fantasies.

I release all sexual fantasies up to my Oversoul to determine their appropriateness.

I trace my sexual fantasies to their point of origin.

I easily determine how my sexual fantasies reflect my relationship with the God-Mind.

Sexual Fidelity

I am sexually faithful to my partner.

I remove myself from any sexual temptations that are inappropriate.

I release any sexually inappropriate thoughts up to my Oversoul.

I use pale red in my root chakra to help maintain sexual fidelity to my partner.

My sexual partner is faithful to me.

I only attract a partner who is sexually faithful to me.

Sexual Intimacy

I attract a partner with whom I feel totally comfortable.

I now have a partner with whom I can be sexually intimate.

I enjoy being sexually intimate with my partner.

I enjoy emotional intimacy during sexual intimacy.

I allow myself to be open and vulnerable during sexual activity.

Trust

I trust myself and therefore I trust others.

I trust others to be kind to me.

I trust others to be loyal and dedicated to me in an emotionally healthy way.

I trust that whatever I give out comes back to me.

I trust everyone with whom I am emotionally involved.

I trust that no one sets out to purposefully hurt me.

I trust the process of life.

I trust my Oversoul and God-Mind.

Unconditional Love

I love myself unconditionally.

My Oversoul and God-Mind love me unconditionally.

I attract people who love me unconditionally.

The outer world reflects unconditional love back to me.

The pale pink of unconditional love permeates every cell and level of my being.

I accept unconditional love into my life.

Upliftment of Humanity

I consider the effects of my words and actions upon the collective consciousness of humanity.

I use my words and actions to uplift the collective consciousness of humanity.

I am a living example that uplifts humanity into new levels of being.

I use my attachment to the Creative Force to uplift humanity.

I use my sexuality to upgrade and uplift humanity into its next positive creative level.

Janet's Articles

Inner Pain/Inner Shame

Everyone who walks this planet has their share of devastating experiences with painful imprints. These events can happen at any juncture of your life, from in utero to childhood through adulthood. These may be conscious memories, or ones that are trying to push through from the subconscious mind. Regardless of origination, they leave their mark, causing a variety of reactions.

Usually whenever anyone experiences pain, there is an underlying fear as well as a feeling of helplessness. Once the feeling of helplessness sets in, then there is often an anger toward whomever the person feels is creating this situation. Anger is part of the "flight or fight" survival mode that is in the Reptilian brain stem. When flight becomes impossible (often motivated by fear), then the remaining choice is to fight, which is often propelled by anger. When the person is in a position where he/she cannot fight—either physically or emotionally restrained, the anger is suppressed into the conscious, and then eventually into the subconscious mind.

As you know, anything that is suppressed gathers strength. All the anger that is suppressed eventually has to come out. Because it is suppressed, it spends a lot of time trying to escape, and as it does, it expresses in a variety of ways.

One way is to lash out at others. People who do this are usually full of pain. They try to clean it out of themselves by giving it to others. If you look under the anger, you will see pain, and under the pain, fear. The deeper the pain, the deeper this type of person tries to inflict it on others in a desperate attempt to get it out of him/herself. Emotional pain lashes out by giving emotional pain to others. Physical pain is common, and in extreme cases rape, mutilations, and even murder.

As one becomes more self-aware, instead of lashing out at others, the tendency is to lash out at oneself. This comes in the form of internal dialogue resulting in low self-worth, self-sabotage, self-denial, and self-degradation. Extreme inner pain may result in anorexia, bulimia, self-mutilation, or even suicide.

Another common reaction to deep inner pain is to numb the pain as it is suppressed. This type of reaction results in not feeling much of anything about anything. People who "numb" the pain operate in one frequency band of emotion without wavering too much one way or the other. To the untrained eye, these people may appear steady and calm, but just beneath the surface lay all the suppressed emotions just waiting to come out. People who are numb to the world often cannot recall unpleasant events, because it is just too painful. Avoidance is easier. Numbing leads to stagnation, or invites a major shakeup through yet another trauma.

Painful experiences frequently lead to feelings of shame, that "I did something wrong and there must be something wrong with me" whether there is or not. Because the imprint is so strong, you may never stop to question it, or if you do, you feel like you cannot move through it. You may feel like you "should have, could have" done something differently to correct the situation. Shame is also a function of low self-worth. The imprint can happen anywhere along the way, but is generally formulated in early childhood. Can you remember the first time that you felt shame?

Be proactive and release these feelings on your own, before something happens in your life to force you into a reactive mode. In other words, take control of the situation now before it builds up to a point where it is in control of you. These emotions all need to be released up to your Oversoul and into God-Mind so that you can move forward into new experiences.

Using the basic techniques, breathe yourself into your center. Check your auric field to determine how far out it extends from your body. With your mind, will it close to your body. Place a violet bubble of protection around it. Now you have boundaries—you know where you start and where you stop. Breathe in from the top of your head to the base of your spine. Exhale up the spine and out through the top of your head, all the way up to your Oversoul. As you do this, feel that you are anchored deep inside of Self, Oversoul, and God-Mind. Within this Triad exists the greatest strength available to you.

As you breathe in with your eyes closed, look within your bubble at the excess red energy of the pain and shame. Breathe it into your center, then using your breath as a tool, exhale it up your spine and right out the top of your head, all the way up to your Oversoul. Watch it flow and flow and flow, repeating this exercise as often as necessary. Watch the excess red energy that comprises pain and shame, and that lives within your auric field, leave. Tell your Oversoul that if there is any specific information that you need to pass it before your inner eye. If anything appears, or memories surface, review and release them. Once you establish this inner work, you can do it anywhere with your eyes wide open—driving, doing household chores, walking, etc.

Whenever you remove something from your auric field, be sure that you replace it, or you will allow what you just released to return. When releasing pain and shame, breathe out the excess red energy and breathe in medium green for emotional healing. Watch it fill your auric field.

As you work through pain and shame, take some time to work on feelings of fear, helplessness, and low self-worth issues in the same way. Breathe them all out through the top of your head, up to your Oversoul and allow anything that you need to see pass before your inner eye. Bring in another color to replace that which you just released.

The deeper you move into your inner Self, there is a greater likelihood that you will encounter the traumas that began the pain and shame in the first place. Develop your releasing skills so that when you finally do reach the core of this work, you can handle whatever you find. Without judgment, label what you find, realizing that it is all a part of experience.

Breaking The Spirit

A motivated person can accomplish absolutely anything—"where there's a will there's a way." A motivated person is creative, innovative, growth-oriented, and expansive. A motivated person knows no boundaries, feeling limitless in his/her possibilities. To a motivated person, "obstacles" do not exist—only signposts that point one in another direction. Motivation is synonymous with knowledge, success, leadership, and power.

A society of motivated people is difficult to control, so the best way to accomplish control is to break their spirit. There are many ways to break the spirit of a people. Once the spirit is broken, and people do not care any more, it is easy to lead them in whatever direction the "spirit breakers" desire.

Think about what happened to the indigenous peoples of North America. They were purposely infected with disease and plied with alcohol. Their food sources were destroyed, they were removed from their natural environments, and their families were split up. Their clothing was changed; their religion was altered, their history tampered with, and their native tongues all but lost. Practically every aspect of their lives was destroyed. Many of them lost their motivation, and along with it, the identity of an entire people.

This has happened throughout history countless times, and is continuing to happen today with all peoples worldwide, most blatantly in the African and Muslim nations.

On a more subtle level, it is happening in the Western world. Look at the colors that are gaining dominance in advertising—slate blue is a color frequency of low oxygenation and depression. Bright red keeps the sexual chakra open, agitated, and ready to receive downloads of ELF. Bright orange is frustrated creativity. Bright yellow matches the pulse waves of ELF, and promotes fear and anxiety. Black covers deep deception and can add to depression. White over-stimulates the nervous system. Observe the colors that surround you from the outside world.

Food, real food that nourishes the body, is becoming increasingly difficult to find. What is passed off as "food" is primarily chemicals, additives, and preservatives. Where's the food?? The media has people so busy looking for "fat" that they forget to look for the food! Most people are overweight and malnourished, or underweight and emaciated. Ethnic food is a rarity; home-cooking an almost-lost art.

Bodies that are not properly cared for cannot function properly. The problem is, this has been such a gradual implementation that most people do not even realize that their bodies are not in great shape. They just keep pushing themselves along under the delusion that they are taking good care of the physical self. What kinds of soul-personalities are drawn to bodies nourished only with artificial foods? How about those willing to accept and supplement with artificial intelligences?

As the planned obsolescence of small business continues, fewer people are motivated to seek meaningful careers, with many opting in to mindless, meaningless work, spending countless hours at jobs that leaves them feeling empty and unfulfilled, waiting for their lives to pass for a few after-work hours of pleasure.

Workers of today are really enslaved by "the company store," no different than days gone by. Most people earn their wages from the same people who own the stores where they shop—so, it is a win-win situation for the few owners of today's commerce. They give their workers a pittance of their worth, then charge tremendous prices at their stores where their workers spend their wages!

Yes, the "little guy" can even be a "stock owner" in the company store (some companies even mandate this) but does he/she ever *really* have any say? Of course not! Only the major shareholders can influence corporate policy. And, when the stocks drop, who loses? Only the "little guy" as their shares are eagerly gobbled up by…who else, but the owners of the "company store!"

On top of giving all their wages to "the company store," they are also perpetually in debt to it as well. Regardless of your credit status, you are made to feel like a pauper via advertisements for debt reduction, bankruptcy, and credit card interest-rate reduction programs.

After you are thoroughly stressed out from being overworked, underpaid, feeling isolated from your family for one reason or another, and failing health, then you are directed to turn to drugs—it does not matter if it is legal or illegal—they are all readily available for your choosing. Forget about any mental work—you do not have time for that. Simply pop a pill for anything from "social anxiety disorder" to sexual dysfunction—you can get a pill from your head to your toes. Many people feel that there is something wrong with them if they are *not* on medication.

Break the spirit of the people. Put them on pills to "make them feel better." Take away their native foods so that the body functions only well enough to get to work and back again. Educate the children only enough so that they can work for others. Make it impossible for small business to exist so that everyone has to work for the "company store." Heck, now they are even working on taking away large vehicles (symbolizing large mind-patterns).

They are clever. They take our blood, sweat, and tears, pay us minimal wages for it, own the company, and then make us spend our paychecks there to further increase their wealth. They want a populace of robots with only just enough spark of life to animate the body; nothing more, nothing less.

Do not let this happen to you! Do not just roll over and wither away. Find the fight within you. Search out what you need for your spirit to thrive. Stand up proudly. Be a way-shower. Positively affect the collective unconscious. Get your space in order on all levels, body, mind, and soul. Listen to your needs. Use your right-brain with guidance from the left-brain. Reach into your self-motivation. Be determined that your spirit will remain motivated and unbroken!

Interdependence: Out of the Silence

"Isolation is one of the major forms of mass mind-control."

How many of you right now feel "alone?" Are you married? Do you have children? Do you go to work every day? Do you belong to organizations and groups? Do you go out shopping? Are you among people? If you answer "yes" to any of these questions, then why do you feel so "alone" among the many varied people with whom you interact every day?

Most likely, you feel alone because you are emotionally isolated. You may desire emotional intimacy, and spend much of your life looking for it, but when you get close, mass mind-control kicks in, not to mention what happens if you are specifically programmed. Something happens to create your immediate emotional withdrawal.

Emotional isolation often begins with the primary caregivers shortly after birth. If the people that you depend upon are not there when you need them you become irate, angry, fearful, and desperate. These feelings are the first walls that you build so that you do not get too close to others. Your justification is that these people "do not understand you." You look for comfort, words of wisdom, and advice from others outside your immediate family.

"Outsiders" eventually disappoint you and again, you withdraw your emotions. Friendships go through their normal ebbs and flows. Love interests throw your emotions about. The job market forces you to be competitive against your colleagues. Emotions continue to isolate. Most religions teach that you are born in sin, relatives try to manipulate you, acquaintances take advantage of you, friends stab you in the back, relationships turn sour, job colleagues become competitive, children disappoint you, big business rips you off, phone menus leave you feeling cold.

The battle of life takes its toll, and "boom!" you are now emotionally isolated from everyone with whom you "should" be intimately connected. Or, perhaps you may just like to refer to this isolation as "freedom" and "independence."

"Independence" can be a lonely place to be. True, you do not have to answer to anyone, but neither do you have a support system of any kind. People who do not feel connected to anyone, anything, or any place are a lot easier to control. Today's society is full of "independent" people.

Few give thoughts these days to "interdependence." This simply means that we all help each other into "win-win" situations. I do something nice for you for no other reason than this is what I choose to give out. If you can help me some day, that is great. If not, someone else will reflect this back to me. I do a something good for you, you do something good for the next person—pass it along. Win-win. The pie of life is limitless. There is enough of everything for everyone. Extend your hand, open your heart and mouth for no other reason than it is the "right thing to do."

Help others for the joy that you feel inside, not for the kudos that you receive from the outside world. If you give to others to receive outside accolades, then you are not "interdependent," but "dependant" upon others for your internal feelings of satisfaction. You then feed your ego, quickly becoming out of balance.

Use discernment—some people are still there to reflect and test your less-than-100% belief in this system. If you play "win-win" with a person who wants to win and wants you to lose, then you need to move on.

Break your own emotional isolation. Speak to others about your feelings. Speak first on the Oversoul level, than test the waters gently. With the strength of your mind-pattern pull your support system to you. Develop your interdependent system. Drop old acquaintances that no longer need to play a part. Release your need for silence and emotional self-isolation. Speak up, speak out.

If the outer world truly does reflect your inner world, then every person that you see is looking for the same things but does not know how to obtain it. You are the one with the tools; therefore you are the teacher, so teach! Some people may move out of your life, but others will move into it that will better reflect the "new" you.

With the release of emotional isolation also comes the release of other emotions that intertwine with it, such as distrust and vulnerability. Recognize that distrust is there to reinforce the emotional isolation. If you distrust others, you will certainly not share your innermost thoughts. If you do speak out, you leave yourself open and vulnerable. If you get hurt, your automatic tendency is to run back inside to hide. If you fall back, this means the powers-that-be win, but you do not.

Are you tired of being alone? Or are these simply words that you use to identify yourself? If you really want to leave this mind-pattern behind, than you will! Release the mind-pattern, replace it with a new mind-pattern, and you are off and running.

Use the following affirmations to help:

I release the need for emotional isolation.

I create an interdependent world where everyone "wins."

With the strength of my mind-pattern, I now have a fantastic support system.

Are you ready to end your emotional isolation? Then come out of your silence to create a strong, interdependent world.

The Sexual Side of Programming

As a general rule, programming is accomplished by opening up the lowest chakra band. This is the easiest entryway into a person's frequency. From the bottom, it is easy to send information up through the chakra system, following the natural flow of a person's psychic energy. During sexual stimulation, this area, a natural conduit for the basic energy of creation, "opens."

It is also this basic energy of creation that is "captured" during sexual rituals and then redirected to create specific manifestations in this reality. This is sometimes referred to as "sexual magick." Whoever controls this sexual energy controls much of what can be created in this reality.

The female becomes like a vacuum as the vagina (or vortex) opens. When penetrated by the male, his energy is sent out through the vortex to create. At the moment of orgasm, directed thought can be propelled into the nonphysical realm to create and bring a physical manifestation into this reality. Symbols may even be visualized or created in the genital area, or the body in general, to enhance the creation process. This is why tattoos, drawings, paintings, and markings are sometimes placed on the body during ritual ceremony. Some people carry this forward into their daily lives, continuing to fulfill their programming. Remember the basic triad of creation—color, tone, and archetype.

This is why the Bible teaches that sex should only be used for procreation. By limiting the masses on what should or should not be done with sexuality, there is little chance that they will discover purposes for sexual energy other than procreation. Brilliantly enough, people privately police themselves in their own bedrooms through guilt.

With the advent of the "sexual revolution," it became more acceptable to have sex for pleasure and the general societal norm became "if it feels good, do it." Again, a distraction for people. While people are busy "feeling good," advertisements, music, televisions shows, and just about everything that you can think of, is geared to keep the sexual chakra band wide open for the insertion of mass mind-control frequencies and ideas. ELF created for these purposes is "piggy-backed" upon these transmissions. This distracts people again from discovering the true purpose of their creative forces.

For those who travel still a different path, there exists one of celibacy. With the mind directed away from the root chakra, there is little chance of these people discovering how to use sexual energy in its higher forms. Or, some of those who may consider themselves "spiritual" may explore such accepted practices as tantra or tantric yoga. These practices actually enhance programming.

People who are specifically targeted for mind-control and programming purposes are usually sexually opened practically upon birth. Children are sexually indoctrinated before they understand what this means. This can mean that they can be sexually stimulated physically, astrally, or via satellite frequency. In some cases, people in the house-hold are participants in the programming.

Because conscious memories may not exist, either because of self-memory blocking due to the trauma, or programming that wipes the conscious mind clear, many of these children grow up with sexual issues. Often this means extremely repressed sexuality, or extremely aggressive sexuality.

Sexual obsessions and fetishes are often the side-effects of programming. Depending upon the predilections, these are clues to how programming was installed, and what kind of programming took place. Because programming often includes pain and pleasure, sadistic/masochistic tendencies are often the residual affects of programming, for example.

158

THE SEXUAL SIDE OF PROGRAMMING

Many programmed people have sexual identity issues. Males may not know if they are homosexual or heterosexual because usually the sexual abuse is perpetuated by another male from an early age. When a person is sexually stimulated in this way, there is no choice but to feel physical pleasure even when the mental aspect is not pleasurable. This is the equivalent to a rape that never stops.

Because the male has felt sexual pleasure literally at the hands of another male, he may grow up thinking that he is sexually attracted to other males. Because of the mind-pattern imprinting, he may feel attracted to men, but not for the reason he consciously concludes. The male may be heterosexual, but because of the imprinting and lack of conscious knowledge of these buried experiences, he assumes he must be homosexual.

Females often spend their lives trying to work out their sexual issues with men. This may lead them into multiple sexual partners or perhaps a life similar to that of a prostitute. Conversely, programming can lead to issues of frigidity and fear of sexual intercourse. Buried subconscious memories of rape may prevent them from a normal sexual relationship with any man.

Female sex slaves may be incapable of feeling pleasure because they are trained to please others, not themselves. Female sex slaves are well-trained to anticipate every detail of any need before it is even expressed by another. This characteristic usually extends beyond sexual activity and into daily life. This type of programming means that she will take care of others even if it is detrimental to her own welfare. This fulfills her programming.

Both men and women often have sexual identity issues—they may consider themselves androgynous because they are so accustomed to being sexually stimulated by both men and women that they do not know to whom they are really attracted. They may even try to emulate a perceived androgynous lifestyle, i.e., the men may grow long hair and appear effeminate while the women may adopt masculine haircuts, body images, and dress. In the extreme case, either gender may live their life as the opposite gender, some even replete with physical operations to enhance the imprinted mind-pattern.

These gender identity issues as well as confusion at how to express these suppressed sexual feelings may lead to no outward expression of sexuality at all. There are many programmed people who have never had a (conscious) sexual experience because of confusion, self-worth issues, sexual natures that have been repressed or even perverted due to imprinting. Because of all the blatant sexual societal bombardment, these people further repress their sexual sides because they think that "everybody is doing it" but them. This is totally untrue, just unspoken, because both men and women are embarrassed to speak of their (conscious) lack of sexual experience.

Many programmed people have difficulty maintaining a monogamous lifestyle because when they have a committed sexual relationship it brings up the issues that they are trying to avoid. Because of the way the programming was conducted, sexual activity brings up those memories. This can make the person uncomfortable, so instead of committing to one person, it is easier to continually try to run away from the issues by frequently changing partners. Lack of a stable relationship enhances the programmers' goal of emotional isolation.

Like everything that exists, sexual activity serves many purposes. Psychic energy, which is the energy that maintains the body (digestion, breathing, walking, etc.), pools at the base of the spine. Orgasm releases this energy back into the system, helping to keep the flow. The auric fields of people who are not sexually active become stagnant, as do their bodies.

Sexual intimacy between two people represents the intimate touching, sharing, and exchanging of the minds. Physically touching someone where you allow no one else to go is a reflection of reaching deep inside your own mind. The longer you stay with a person and explore your mutual mental houses, the more this is reflected in your mutual sexual sharing.

However, programmed people often shy away from this type of intimacy because it brings up uncomfortable memories. Rather than run away from them, use the brown merger symbol at the pineal gland during sexual activity. Allow the memories to surface, merging them into the system and releasing them to your Oversoul as they surface.

Alters may surface during sexual activity for either sex. Be aware when alters surface and integrate them. Keep notes on these experiences in your deprogramming journal. This is all part of your path, whether you or your partner consciously want it to be. Rather than avoid it, bring the information out.

Maintaining a sexual relationship with one person helps keep continued sexual abuse and exploitation away. Within a monogamous sexual relationship, every time you have sexual intercourse, you imprint each other with your frequencies. This helps to keep others from encroaching on your frequencies, as well as prevent others from continuing to imprint you astrally or via satellite. As an analogy, think about buying a house. Before you buy it, the more times you visit the house, the more your specific energies are in the house. This precludes the energies of others, helping to ensure that no one else buys the house.

During general deprogramming exercises, you may feel sexually stimulated. This means that you are opening up sexually and are vulnerable to outside influence. This is the time to engage in sexual activity with your committed partner. Because your frequencies are monitored, your handlers know when you are sexually stimulated. This is when you will receive extra ELF bombardment. They also know when you actually participate in sexual intercourse. Again, this opens you up and makes you vulnerable to others' control, so use hyperspace protection techniques.

Remember, you can only be programmed with what you already are. If you are a part of creation in some way, use this for your benefit, instead of allowing others to use it against you. By integrating your training, turn something negative into something positive. Make it work for you. Consciously integrate your sexual training to upgrade your sexual activity with a committed partner.

Understand the energetic circuit that is created between male and female during sexual activity. Learn about sexuality as it is intended to be. Understand that the various sexual positions all have layers of meaning. Explore "sexual magick" in accordance with the wishes of your Oversoul and God-Mind. Explore the mental and physical intimacy that is created between two people. Explore sexuality on a grander scale. Understand that it is all about creation, and the orgasmic release of energy is your opportunity to create in this reality.

Keep the root chakra in pale red with violet protection around this area specifically if you suspect that you are still being compromised. If you have a partner, tie your energies together here—use a pale red cord with violet around the cord between the two of you. Look for gray, bright yellow, or bright red energy—any kind of invasive energy that is not natural to this chakra band. Trace it if you can so that you can stop it. Trace the source when you feel sexually stimulated. Determine if these feelings originate from within yourself or if you are being artificially stimulated.

Avoid anything that stimulates you from the astral levels, as this will pull you into alters, or open you up to allow your sexual energies to be utilized by others. Bear in mind that if this happens, there is a part of you that invites this in. Find the mind-pattern that allows this so you can correct it.

Anyone can have sex. An animal can have sex. Sex alone ties people to the astral levels. During sexual rituals, people are trained to have sex with astral entities, animals, specific partners, and multiple partners of both sexes. Sex is one of the strongest forces of the universe, ensuring self-perpetuation of life in this reality.

During deprogramming, sexual issues are prevalent because most programming is accomplished through sexual activity. You have to undo the process in much the same way as it was originally accomplished. The sexual chakra is extremely misunderstood and misused in a way that ties people into lower astral activity. When a person is committed to "feeling good" only, the true purpose of sexuality is totally overlooked.

Programmed people often feel quite sexual and this is expressed in the auric field, which means others respond to the open sexual chakra. This can mean covert/overt sexual attention from others (including rape and sexual abuse), feelings of being particularly sexually attractive to others, and so on. This is part of the programmed person's identity, whether they consciously know it or not, because this is part of the training. Others react to the auric field, including the colors and symbolism contained within it.

During deprogramming the integration of these sexual aspects back into the system can be traumatic, not only from memories but because there are parts of the person that does not want to give up this sexual identity. In some aspects, the sexual identity is the only identity. Without it, the conscious part feels lost and useless.

Sexual fantasies are often the key to programming, what you were used for, and what was done to you. You are programmed to want specific behaviors, so even if your logical mind finds certain acts repulsive, these same thoughts may trigger specific sexual reactions/ stimulation. This is the same as the old story of Pavlov's dog. You ring a bell and the dog salivates. If you suspect that you are programmed, try to remember your earliest childhood sexual fantasies. These are definite clues to your programming. Anything that may seem bizarre may actually have its origin in programming.

There are several general points on the body that are used for implantation and storing cellular information. On these male, these are generally the pineal gland area, under the arms, nipples, naval, penis, scrotum, and anus. These are also the easiest places to release information. On the female, cellular information is stored most often in the pineal gland, mouth, ear lobes, neck, breasts/nipples, naval, and vagina. Stimulating any of these areas releases stored information. Use the pineal gland as a screen to view the released information.

Two committed partners can help each other to deprogram during sexual intercourse. You can also deprogram yourself through sexual self-manipulation. The difficulty with this is that because of the type of information which surfaces, it is easy for a person to stop. A male can deprogram a male, because as one emits the information, the other does not absorb it. A male can deprogram a female because he will not absorb what she emits. As an aside, this is why it is not appropriate for a female to have a multitude of sexual partners—she absorbs the male's semen, and thus is imprinted with his genetics and programming. Males, on the other hand, do not get imprinted by females.

A female cannot deprogram a female because one would absorb what the other emits. Once the deprogramming process starts, there needs to be some kind of conclusion, such as an orgasm, to seal the person's energy—otherwise he/she remains open.

Self-deprogramming, or deprogramming with a committed partner, is the safest way to proceed. Go at your own pace, keeping a detailed journal. Cautiously, but steadily, keep yourself balanced at every turn so that you do not trigger alters. You will find your way into another layer of Self. As with everything you do, appreciate the process.

The Original Orgasmic "Big Bang" of Creation

Imagine the vastness of the God-Force imploding within Itself, and then exploding Itself with an orgasmic release so tremendously explosive and magnificently thunderous that all physical realities simultaneously manifest. This is the Original Act of Creation of God-Mind creating within and from Itself. This is the Original Androgynous Creation from which all else flows. This *is* the Original Sexual Magick Act.

On the inbreath of implosion, Oversoul streams of creative force manifest within the God-Mind. These streams of creation contain all that God-Mind needs for androgynous manifestation. To create the largest, most magnificent expulsion from Itself possible, It rearranges Itself so that the Original Act of Creation occurs.

Within this rearrangement are six easily identifiable energy streams necessary to create the most powerful explosion possible (refer to diagram page 168):

• Thruster energy streams that send the manifestations out into physical reality.

• Battery or "booster" energy streams that provide the power.

• Conduit or "bridge" energy streams for the power to reach the thruster energy streams.

- "Absorb and store power" energy streams.

- Conduit or "bridge" energy streams for the "absorb/store power" energy streams to reach the thruster energy streams.

- Balance energy streams for the thruster energy streams.

The above energy streams are described linearly, but in True Reality, this all happens simultaneously. Go to your Oversoul with this information and ask that a visual come into your mind to truly understand this Original Act of Creation. Visualize all of the above occurring simultaneously.

After the explosion, these energy streams filter down into physical realities through the Oversoul levels. Oversouls express the wide variation of sexual orientations through the multitude of soul-personalities that they create. They are in their own way basically heterosexual, homosexual, bisexual, or asexual. Extrapolating this further, each soul-personality carries forth the sexual characteristics that his/her own Oversoul wishes to explore for the God-Mind. Soul-personalities that descend from:

- Thruster energy streams express as heterosexual.

- Battery/booster energy streams express as gay males.

- Conduit/bridge energy streams for the battery/booster energy streams express as bisexual males.

- Absorb/store power energy streams express as lesbian females.

- Conduit/bridge energy streams for absorbed/stored power energy streams express as bisexual females.

- Balance energy streams for thruster energy streams express as asexual.

All energy streams are necessary. None are more or less important. All are equal in value to the overall process. If people truly understood their innate sexual natures via their Original Creative Energy Stream, physical realities would automatically be in balance, as each soul-personality would express him/herself in total alignment with his/her Original Creative Frequency.

Because there are so many mixed outside sexual influences, few people are truly in alignment with their own Original Creative Frequency. Those who are in touch with this aspect of Self risk being ostracized by society if their Original Creative Frequency happens to be something other than heterosexual.

Heterosexuality is promoted for the perpetual procreation of a slave race. Heterosexuality is also promoted as the "norm" to keep people from aligning with their own Original Creative Frequency. In addition, the promotion of heterosexuality prevents people from coming together to perform Sexual Magick as it was Originally intended.

Within God-Mind, all things are acceptable and encouraged without judgment or criticism. Soul-personalities are at liberty to explore every creative energy stream if so desired. Freewill exists on all levels for every aspect of life. As a microcosm of the macrocosm, you explore yourself as God-Mind explores Itself. As you learn about who and what you are, God-Mind learns about who and what It is. As above, so below. You are a continuation of an extremely fascinating process. Keep this in mind the next time you experience the "big bang" of orgasmic release.

The Original Sexual Magick Act

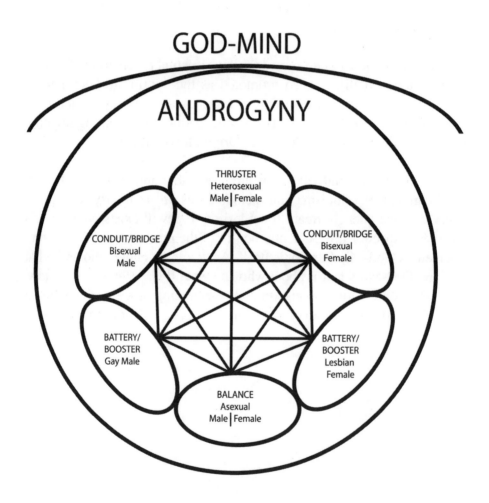

Sexual Dream Dictionary

A

Abortion: Stopping a new idea from coming to fruition.

Airplane: Alter groups about to be activated to higher level.

Androgyny: Being neutral or non-committal.

Anus: Releasing capabilities of the past.

Apple, becomes a plum: Ovarian symbol/dangerous choice for activation.

Archway: Sexual desires or yearnings.

B

Bed: Putting old ideas to rest.

Bedroom: Altered state.

Bedroom, Father's old: Spiritual idea not used.

Bicycle: Subliminal sexuality; sexual activity moving forward.

Bisexuality: Balancing logic with emotions.

Blanks, shooting: Infertility.

Blood: Joy of life.

Breasts, large: Feeling a large need to give to others.

Breasts, more than one: A need to give more than you should to others.

Breasts, small: Feeling as if you do not need to give to others

Brother: Booster or battery for energy, alters in same group, alter with related personality.

Brother's friend: Another personality of the same Oversoul.

Brown: Grounding and balance.

Building, roof of: Moving outside of construct.

Bull's eye(on breasts): Need to be nurtured.

C

Chest: Emotional connection.

Children, few: Some new ideas.

Children, grown: Ideas that are no longer present or useful.

Church: Established spiritual beliefs, fixed/controlled spiritual ideas.

Church(was a bar/club): Playing with spirituality.

Church (cash/casino check): Your spiritual ideas cannot be applied now.

Clitoris: A need for stimulation creatively.

Cunnilingus: Preparing physical environment for a creative energy.

D

Disintegrating: Femininity is being lost.

Doorways: Connection to various alter groupings/families.

Dress, white: Cleansing what you show to others.

E

Earth: Mother energy.

Egg: Undeveloped idea for physical reality.

Egg, fertilized: Developing idea in physical reality.

F

Family: Soul group.

Father: God-Mind within you.

Fellatio: Absorbing God-Mind power.

Female child: Logical idea that needs to be developed.

Fetus: Beginning of a new idea or concept; ideas that were never given a chance for completion.

G

Gay male: A step-up of energy for the God-Mind; creative forces.

Girl: Left-brain/personality.

Group sex: Recycling powerful creative energies.

Gun: Phallic symbol, penis.

Guy: God-Mind within.

Gym: Need to strengthen.

Gypsy: A wandering mind-pattern; unfocused direction.

H

Hard to swallow: Domination sequence.

Having sex while others watch: Need for support in merging self or balancing.

Having sex with same sex: Amplifying (male) or absorbing (female) creative energy.

Heart, being drained: Emotions removed to perform function.

High security: Self-protection; feeling vulnerable.

Hispanic men: Exciting ideas of a creative nature.

Homeless: Moving consciousness outside of the Oversoul.

Horse: Message.

House: Oversoul/personality.

House, buying: New soul-personality characteristics.

House, furnished: Thoughts in the soul-personality.

House, to the left: Left-brain; ego personality.

Hundred-dollar bill: Total awareness of God-Mind.

Husband, without: Not balanced; lack of creativity or emotion.

K

Kiss a girl: Merging.

Kissing: Balancing ideas between masculine and feminine aspects; for programmed individuals, merging of two programs.

L

Labia: Protection your creative inputs.

Left, second from: Balancing ego or left-brain.

Lesbian female: Absorbing and manipulating physical energies.

Lipstick: Masking words...what color?

Lots of people: Personality aspects.

Lush trees: Rich family history.

Lying on top: Taking control.

M

Magenta: Anger in the love emotions.

Male child: Creative idea that needs to be developed.

Mall: Many choices in life.

Man(in suit): Oversoul.

Man(sat down on chair): Alters taking your place.

Man, older, fat: Guardian.

Man, very stern: Internal programmer.

Maroon: Courage.

Masturbation: Self-love; expressing God-Mind within.

Mattress spring: Activation of dormant alter.

Men: Right-brain; intuitive ideas.

Men, older: Strong guardian alter.

Menstruation: Clearing out creative ideas; feeling unclean.

Migrant: Unstable ways.

Mini Casinos: Taking chances with each choice.

Model: Perfect logic.

Moon: Female issues and ideas; hidden control issues or something that has been hidden; astral energies.

Motel: Temporary condition.

Mother: Original left-brain/ego ideas of self.

Mountains: Raising levels.

Mouth, into: Need to absorb information.

Mouth, roof of: Information specifically for future.

N

Naked, nude: Exposing self to the world.

Nipples: Programming trigger; need for nurturing.

Numbers 1-12: Fragment personalities with construct.

Nurses: Need to heal the ego issues.

Nuts, bolts, testicles: Sexual power toward creation, i.e., sexual magick.

O

Old dancers/cheerleaders: Foundational enthusiasm from left-brain thinking; self-encouragement for old ideas.

Old lady: Ego-thinking; left-brain.

Old teachers: Original thought patterns that directed you.

One-story: Surface layer of meaning.

Open door: Vortex.

Operations, sexual: Altering creative/emotional issues.

Ovaries: A pool of ideas that is not yet time to be created.

Over-the-hill women: Thoughts from the ego that are no longer valid.

Own hands: In current life.

P

Paramedics, male: Creativity/emotion.

Parents: Old, left-brain, right-brain ideas that guide one.

Party: Group of alters coming together.

Passengers, slid off: Removing personality aspects that no longer suit you.

Penis: Power of creativity and God-Mind.

Peter: Fixed sexual ideas pertaining to male figures.

Phallic symbols: Power; God-Mind strength; need for sexuality.

Plum: Uterine symbol.

Poison gas: Negative emotions that you avoid.

Pornography: Basis for underlying mind-pattern.

Pounds (300): Creating twinning program.

Pregnant: Ready to create a new idea; holding onto creative issues without releasing them.

Previously hidden: Subconscious awareness coming to the surface.

Prince William: Illuminati prototype-function.

Princess Diana: New World Religion icon.

Princess of Wales: Mother Goddess of Ceremony.

Psychology building: Mental fixations.

R

Rape: Forced merger of left-brain/right-brain.

Realtor, male: Aspect of right-brain that helps to search for answers.

Reception room: Pineal gland function.

Rectum: See anus.

Red carpet: Energy coming into brain for alters.

Red/$5: Need to heal anger.

Red hair: Uses anger as strength.

Relatives: Aspects of self/personality pieces.

Right arm: What one is able to grasp right now about spiritual and creative ideas.

Right to left: Going from mental to physical.

S

Semen: Creative juices flowing; imprinting ideas on others.

Sex: Need to blend or merge left-brain with right-brain.

Shower: Need for a cleansing or refreshing situation.

Sleep: Downloading information.

Sleep away: Buried memories.

Snowed overnight: Cleaning and cleansing negativity.

Snuggle: Preliminary energy for merging left-brain/right-brain.

Spaceship: Higher awareness.

Space toilet: Eliminating spiritual ideas that no longer serve you.

Sun: God-mind; masculine ideas; shedding light on a topic.

T

Testicles: Twinning programming; creating spiritually and physically.

Toilet: Completely eliminating the past.

Two-lane road: Left-brain, right-brain.

U

Uterus: Planning something; developing ideas; holding creative patterns.

V

Vagina: Holding and receiving creative energies.

W

Waist deep: Sexual/creative issues.

Waves: Turbulence in life.

Water: Represents your life.

Wet Sand: Unstable balancing.

Whales: Big problems in life.

White: Cleansing; purity.

Woman: Left-brain; ego self.

Woman, (in crimson): Anger at physical reality.

Woman, wrapped in carpet: Abduction/control of logic.

Woman, older, dead: End of egotistical thinking.

Woman priest: Concept of loving physical reality more than spirituality.

Womb: See uterus.

Y

Young wife: Newer logical ideas.

Glossary

Alter: Section or compartmentalized personality within a programming matrix.

Androgynous: Male and female combined without sexual distinction.

Archetype: Symbol or glyph from hyperspace or mind-patterns.

Astral Plane: The border zone between physical reality and hyperspace.

Bisexual: Sexually desiring both males and females.

Ceremony: Gathering to celebrate or honor an entity or Illuminati holiday.

Chakra band: Energy center of the body and encompassing area.

Chakras: Along the human spinal column, there are seen main nerve bundles, called ganglions, which are esoterically called chakras, a word which means "wheels" in Sanskrit. They form along the "S" curve of the spine which looks like a snake. For this reason, the chakra system is referred to as Kundalini, the Sanskrit word for snake.

Cunnilingus: Orally stimulating the female genitalia.

Deprogramming: Techniques to block and/or remove mind-control/ programming.

ELF: Extra low frequency generally related to microwaves for mind-control purposes.

Fantasy, sexual: Describes your true relationship to God-Mind.

Fellatio: Orally stimulating male genitalia.

Fetish: Peculiar sexual act or body part that stimulates a person.

Frequency: A rate of vibration that distinguishes one flow of energy from all other flows.

God-Mind: Neutral energy; All That Is.

Group-mind: Formed when vibrations band together.

Hybrids: Mixed genetics from two or more species to create a new species.

Hyperspace: A region of consciousnes which exists outside of linear space and time.

Illuminati: Member or associate of one of the 13 ruling families on Earth.

Intersex: Having the physical characteristics of both male and female genitalia; formerly known as "hermaphrodites."

Language of Hyperspace: The Original Language that emanates from the Mind of God consisting of color, tone, and archetype.

Love: Neutral energy that emanates from God-Mind that does not discriminate.

Lyrae: Star system in the Milky Way Galaxy that is the origin point for all humans.

Macrocosm: God-Mind; All That Is; the larger picture of everything.

Masochism: Sexual pleasure derived from having absolutely no control over what is done to you; a need/desire to be hurt.

Microcosm: You; a world in miniature.

Mind-Pattern: Blueprint of a person's thoughts.

New World Order (N.W.O.): Global government dictatorship being created by the Illuminati.

Oversoul: Your point of origin out of God-Mind; the larger part of the Self.

Polyamory: Loving many; a lifestyle where a group comprised of both males and females develop intimate relationships with each other, including sexual relationships.

Programming, sexual: Involves the use of sexuality and the stimulation of the genitals and other sensitive body parts for the purpose of creating functions and alters within the fragmented mind.

Psychic energy: Your personal energy; nonphysical energy that the mind and body generate.

Reptilian: A being with lizard-like characteristics from either the inner Earth or Draco star system.

Sadism: Deriving sexual pleasure from giving pain.

Sexual Magick: Process that brings forth a specific manifestation into this reality for a specific purpose via use of sexual techniques.

Sexual trigger: Word, action, color, etc. that stimulates a sexual programmed function.

Simultaneous time: All events occurring at the same instant.

Soul-personality: Individual strand of an Oversoul.

Species-mind: Created when similar frequencies band together.

Standard Array: Implants placed in strategic parts of the body to facilitate mind-control and programming.

Transgender: A person of one sex who feels like the opposite sex but does not physically change the body.

Transsexual: A person who physically alters the body from one gender to another.

True Reality: The absolute state of being.

Universal energy: Energy that is available to everyone; emanates from God-Mind.

Universal Law: Rules and regulations that pervade all creation; emanates form God-Mind.

Vibration: Frequency rate of an energy.

Visualization: Creating a mental scenario that can be manifested either mentally or physically; centered at the pineal gland.

dysfunction, sexual 151

E

Earth
  12, 14, 61, 67, 69, 94, 119, 171, 180
Earth, inner 181
effeminate 159
effort, conscious 19
egg 14, 21, 62, 65, 107, 171
egg, fertilized 107
egg, fertilized in Womb 107
eggs 12
ego 45, 154, 174
ego, balancing 172
ego-thinking 174
egotistical 96
Egypt 71
Egyptian, Ancient 29
Egyptians 66
ejaculate 12, 13, 129, 134
ejaculated 74, 78
ejaculates 67
ejaculation
  14, 53, 67, 78, 80, 108, 134
ejaculation, oral 67
ejaculation, premature 53, 134
ejaculations 92
ejection 14
electrodes 74, 76
elements, four of the Earth 68
elevate 137
ELF 150, 158, 180
elite 72
emaciated 150
embarrassed 160
embarrassment 24
emotional 41, 155
emotional, parental abuse 88
emotionally 45, 143
emotions 16, 84, 120, 169, 171
emotions, love 172
emotions, negative 175
empathy 48
empowered 86
empowerment 49, 107
empty 36, 87, 150
emulate 22

encounter, sexual 41
encounters, sexual 44, 52
enemies 44
enemy 45
energies, astral 68, 173
energies, creative 15, 35, 171
energies, dark 60
energies, nonphysical 12
energies, nurturing 52
energies, sexual 91
energy 29
energy, balance streams 166
energy, battery booster streams 166
energy, booster streams 165
energy, bridge streams 165
energy, creation 16
energy, creative 12, 86, 170, 171
energy, creative stream 167
energy, feminine 12
energy, masculine 12, 139
energy, mother 171
energy, neutral 44, 180
energy, nonphysical 181
energy of creation 157
energy, personal 31
energy, personal integrity 91
energy, psychic 31, 157, 160, 181
energy, psychic flow 31, 32
energy, psychic lines 34
energy, red 147
energy, sexual
  24, 31, 36, 40, 157, 158
energy, thruster streams 165, 166
energy, universal 182
enforcement, law 57
engaged 57
enslaved 17, 150
enthralled 17
entities, astral 24, 74, 162
entity 67, 179
entity, astral 66, 67
entity, demonic/astral 67
entryway 157
environment 13, 65, 110
enzyme 63
equipment, torture 67
erection 53, 78

INDEX

INDEX

M

machines, slot 24
macrocosm 15, 35, 167, 181
magenta 172
Magick, Sexual
    157, 161, 167, 174, 181
Magick, Sexual Ritual
    36, 63, 69, 76, 80, 86, 89, 91, 96
Magick, Sexual Ritual ceremony 128
Magick, Sexual Rituals 65, 66
makeup 24, 29
makeup artists 23
male
    13, 16, 21, 45, 47, 52, 53, 61, 65,
78, 95, 172
male, erect genitalia 14
male, feminized 30
male, programmed 78
male-to-male 96
male/female, standard body 98
males
    12, 14, 29, 35, 45, 56, 58, 68, 159
males, bisexual 166
males, semi-naked 22
mall 173
malnourished 150
man 21, 45, 63, 173
manifest 14
manifestation
    15, 51, 52, 65, 69, 91, 96, 117, 119
manifestation, androgynous 165
manifestation, physical
    67, 68, 74, 134, 140, 157
manifestations 94
manifestations, physical 59, 140
manifestations, specific 157
manifesting 13
manifests 56
manipulate 49, 64, 154
manipulated 66
manipulation
    43, 44, 48, 50, 66, 138, 139
manipulation, monetary 48
manipulations, time 120
manipulators 48
marketplace 18
markets, meat 39

markings 157
marks, stretch 63
maroon 173
marriage 23
marriages, group 93
married 57, 153
masculine 29, 47, 86
masochism 86, 181
masses 94, 98
master 73
masters 67
masturbate 59, 63, 79, 139
masturbation 35, 36, 173
mat, performance 67
materialistic 96
materials, DNA 52
matrix, Oversoul 41
matrix, programming 179
matters, creative 52
mattress 173
maturation, psychological 98
meanings, double 68
media 18, 21, 25, 37, 40
meditation 36
memories 81, 133, 147
memories, buried 176
memories, conscious 145, 158
memories, programming/ceremony 87
memories, sexual 102
memories, subconscious 159
memories, uncomfortable 160
memory, cellular 84, 133
memory, cellular/subconscious 86
memory, genetic 86
men 19, 39
men, Hispanic 172
menopause 12
menstrual cycles 28
menstrual, monthly cycle 35
menstruation 173
mental 41
mentality, victimization 84
merge 13, 61, 176
merger, brown 76
merger, brown symbol 160
merges 80
merging 52, 171, 172

INDEX

INDEX

INDEX

INDEX

www.stewartswerdlow.com
www.janetswerdlow.com
www.expansions.com

Visit the *Expansions* website to read the
latest up-to-date information on:

Daily Practical Tips
Current Event & News Postings
Stewart's Column: *StewartSays...*
Janet's Articles: *Belief Systems Shattered*
Janet's Column: *Dear Friends*
Dream Center
Life Support Group ™ **and Leader Contacts**
Latest Books, Videos, & Products
Seminars, Lectures, & Events
Contributing Authors...and Much More!